£8.37
ROSE
D.

YEOVIL COLLEGE
STUDY CENTRE
TO BE RETURNED OR RENEWED BY THE DATE
LAST STAMPED BELOW

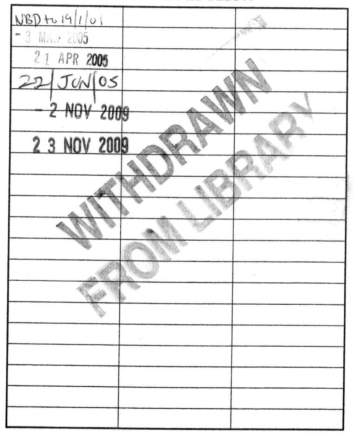

ACTING
A Drama Studio Source Book

JOHN MILES-BROWN

PETER OWEN
LONDON AND CHESTER SPRINGS

PETER OWEN LIMITED
73 Kenway Road, London SW5 0RE

Peter Owen books are distributed in the USA by Dufour Editions Inc.,
Chester Springs, PA 19425-0007

First published in Great Britain 1985
Reprinted 1987, 1990
© John Miles-Brown 1985
This edition published 2000

ISBN 0 7206 1094 X

A catalogue record for this book is available from the British Library

Printed and bound in Great Britain by MPG Books Ltd, Bodmin, Cornwall

y0067626

To Barbara

CONTENTS

L.

Introduction

The aim of this book is to provide a range of ideas for practical work in the drama studio. These acting exercises, because of their inherent flexibility, variety of possible interpretations and the fact that they deal with basic dramatic problems, are suitable for use with a wide range of students from secondary education and youth drama to drama societies, drama schools, communication courses in colleges of further education, colleges of higher education, polytechnics and universities.

Drama is frequently regarded as a rather specialized recreational activity, of interest to only a minority of people. Yet the dramatic instinct is basic to human nature. From the earliest times – the age of the ancient Greek dithyramb (an act of worship in honour of Dionysus) – to the present day, from the rituals of primitive societies to the great Shakespearean tragedies and the sophisticated works of contemporary dramatists like Jean Genet, Samuel Beckett, John Osborne, Arthur Miller, Edward Albee, Harold Pinter, Alan Ayckbourn and Tom Stoppard, drama has been used as a means of understanding, gaining control over, challenging or coming to terms with the human condition. There is a thirst, a need for drama. The mass of dramatic material broadcast on television and radio has a regular audience of millions. Theatres and cinemas offer a large variety of plays and films. It is also interesting to note that many events in the sporting world contain some of the most powerful ingredients of drama, such as conflict, contrast, spectacle, suspense, timing and physical skills.

9

I have always found it profitable to attempt to demonstrate to students how they quite unconsciously use some of the techniques of drama during the course of an average day. All of us, unless we are incredibly dull and inflexible, can project a range of personalities to deal with particular situations. An example is a young acquaintance of mine who leaves home for his work in the City of London very smartly dressed in a dark suit, clean shirt, expensive-looking tie, briefcase and umbrella – the image of what his city employers would wish him to be. On return from work all the trappings of a young city gent are immediately discarded and a costume change reveals a very casual, deliberately scruffy person in grubby training shoes, old jeans, a tee-shirt with a lurid emblem on the chest, a different hairstyle and an earring. He has changed his personality to correspond to the image that his friends will find acceptable. So, in the act of dressing for the occasion, we are role-playing. We dress 'up' and we dress 'down'. We dress for the role we have to play in life at a particular moment. Clothes reveal a great deal about a person. They can convey a considerable amount of information that would often surprise the wearer. The private person inside the costume may differ, intentionally or unintentionally, from the image that the outer garb projects. The posture of the body within the clothing can also be very revealing. It can tell the observer something about a person's general physical condition, possible age and probable state of mind, for example. Posture can reinforce the statement made by the clothes worn, or else contradict it. We hear of someone being able to 'carry off' a shabby or unsuitable garment because the carriage and personality compensate for the inappropriate costume. We see people wearing splendid clothes which are sometimes negated by poor posture. The dress of the average person and the costume of the actor both help to create a mental image of a certain personality for the wearer. Clothes and other masking devices that we use to cover our nakedness – including moustaches, beards, spectacles and jewellery – condition our view of ourselves and thus influence personality.

In our everyday encounters we make constant subtle adjustments to our projected image, according to the circumstances in which we find ourselves. Not only do we dress to suit the occasion, but we adjust our posture, gestures, voice, speech and use of eye contact according to the image we wish, perhaps quite unconsciously, to transmit to those with whom we are dealing. Consider the difference between the salesman selling you a secondhand car, who is deliberately using his act of enthusiasm, motoring expertise, friendliness, even flattery to get your cash and the same salesman when you return the car a few days later and demand your money back in full, because you have discovered it is falling apart with rust and must have done many more miles than is shown on the speedometer. His personality will almost certainly change in an instant. He will distance himself from you, appear uninterested, possibly be rude, try to downgrade you and upgrade himself; he will use a different style of gesture and movement, voice and speech. His technique is used as a means of self-preservation. We can say 'good morning' to people in a variety of different ways. We sit with our friends in the pub using tone, gesture, eye contact and even language that is markedly different from that which we use when attending a formal dinner with strangers. We are all actors. The task is to develop and train these faculties to communicate to an audience the thoughts and characteristics created by a free-flowing imagination.

At an early stage in drama courses I have often found it highly instructive to send students out on a field trip to make a study of people as they go about their daily business. A high street is a good place to track down quarry. Students are asked to seek out, study and report back on two contrasting characters. The task is to observe them closely, but not too closely – as one student was severely clouted after trailing someone too obviously. The students are asked: to note sex, estimate age and physical condition; to consider how the sex, apparent age and physical condition appeared to influence movement and gesture; to indicate what they thought the clothing revealed about the character; to say whether movement and manner were in accord with the clothes; to note characteristics and mannerisms; to try to guess occupation, status and life style; to listen to voice and speech and note what they revealed; and, finally, to note the character's attitude and to comment on whether this was reflected in both voice and movement. When the students have had time to think about their two characters, they are asked to describe them as vividly as possible to the rest of the group and then to characterize them, using movement, gesture, voice and speech to recreate incidents which show the contrast between them.

Inevitably, drama training today is based to a large degree on the work and writings of Konstantin Stanislavski, whose 'system' is still the best reasoned approach to the work of the actor. Writers such as Diderot, Appia, Craig and Coquelin had contributed theories on the art of dramatic performance, but, until Stanislavski had made a study in depth of the actor's work and evolved what he called his 'system', no framework had existed within which an actor could prepare himself or herself with such thoroughness. However, as Stanislavski pointed out, the 'system' is not something to be acted, it is a means whereby the mind and body can be prepared to allow the talents of the individual actor to emerge. Bertolt Brecht, Antonin Artaud and Jerzy Grotowski all expressed ideas about the nature of the actor's performance and, although sometimes these may appear contradictory, each aims in its own way to guide the actor towards that essential quality, a sense of dramatic truth appropriate to a character in a particular mode of production.

Stanislavski required actors to be physically free; to develop powers of imagination and concentration; to believe in the characters within the stage situation; to work from conscious techniques in order to liberate subconscious reactions (the psycho-technique); to prepare themselves mentally and physically; to train their memory; to stimulate their emotional memory; to react to the given stage circumstances as if they were true, but of course in a controlled way; to discover the ruling idea of a role; to have a series of objectives for each unit of the performance, leading to the realization of the super-objective; to develop empathy and communicate fully; and to use make-up, properties, costume, setting and effects to reinforce their characterizations. This summary of Stanislavski's objectives may look formidable, but good actors do much of this instinctively and others learn to do it over a period of time. My own view is that it is best to allow students to acquire basic techniques of relaxation, voice, speech and movement and to gain confidence through carefully monitored improvisational work, without demanding that they adhere to a 'system'. Then, when a groundwork of basic technique has been acquired, as well as a degree of confidence, one can more fruitfully discuss the theories of Stanislavski and others.

The exercises in this book have been devised to provide situations in which drama students can come to grips with a variety of techniques within the experimental atmosphere of a studio. Some you may recognize as being the staple diet of drama training, as they reflect enduring aspects of human nature that must be explored. Most of the improvisation ideas are presented in the form of a problem that has to be solved in dramatic terms. All this material can be freely modified by the drama tutor to suit the aptitudes of particular students, the temperaments of the groups and the physical conditions of work. Furthermore, exercises invented by the tutor for specific groups should prove rewarding.

Concerning equipment, it is a good idea to have in reserve a stock of chairs, a few armchairs and a sofa or two, tables, old telephones and a wide collection of properties such as screens, drapes, hats, shawls, wigs, sticks, bells and anything else that may prove to be a stimulus to the imagination. Small properties can be mimed as part of the exercise. However, a tangible property is often the talisman that helps to provide a sense of dramatic truth and, consequently, confidence within the actor.

The first section deals with relaxation, because relaxation is a fundamental requirement for the performer. It enables the performer's mind, body and voice to be flexible and responsive to dramatic stimuli. A tense performer cannot communicate easily and is aware of self and not the character in the situation. It is suggested that all sessions start with some form of relaxation. After a time, when the techniques are familiar, students can carry out their own routines for a few minutes.

All drama work must have an aim. In improvisation the work can sometimes become haphazard. Therefore, for each improvisation there must be at least one stated aim in view – the development of character, character relationships, timing, the situation, creating the atmosphere, aspects of movement, dramatic climax, projection or use of the acting area, for example.

An essential ingredient in all this work is that it must be enjoyable. The tutor, like the director, must generate the right sort of atmosphere to permit full creativity together with a sense of self-discipline that comes from the students' concentration and the tutor's level of expectancy.

1

Relaxation

Relaxation is fundamental for the efficient use of the body, not only in drama, but in carrying out our daily routines with maximum efficiency. Much of what is said about the inhibiting factors of physical tension – lack of relaxation – may be applied to mental tensions, for the mind and body should operate in harmony. A confident and relaxed state of mind will normally be reflected in a more relaxed use of the physique and should encourage a state of mental and physical equilibrium in which the imagination can trigger physical responses to dramatic stimuli. In drama the term 'being relaxed' does not mean being muscularly slack, but being in that state of well-being when the muscles of the body are so tuned that no unnecessary tension is hampering movement, breathing or voice production and the whole body is able to function at an optimum level. When an actor is relaxed, all that we might notice is that his or her performance appears natural, dramatically true and convincing; the vocal tone is full and flexible, movement and gesture are free and expressive and respond to the demands of the stage situation. On the other hand, when an actor is tense the results are usually obvious. The vocal tone is hard and lacking in range, breathing is shallow and the voice may not project, movement is restricted and possibly awkward. Also, the actor cannot easily relate to the fellow members of the cast because mental and physical tension is concentrating attention on his or her own body, leading to difficulty in communicating.

Tension in a performer can be transmitted to other members

of the cast, in fact to the audience itself, although not many members of the audience would be able to pinpoint why that particular performer gives them a sense of unease. A noticeable way in which tension can be transmitted is by a tense and strident vocal tone. A speaker who uses the voice in this way not only fails to communicate fully, because listeners become irritated, but the tension can be transferred to the muscles of the throat. Tension usually shows itself first in the voice, because the breathing is often shallow and the muscles of the larynx are tensed as for the production of a range of higher notes. Further, there is little resonance, as the resonating cavities of the pharynx and chest are muscularly restricted and the oral cavity is not open enough to add resonance and give projection.

Part of the difficulty in inducing relaxation is that some people are tense most of the time. Various factors can lead to this state. The pace and stresses of modern life, the noise with which many of us are surrounded – trains, cars, motorbikes, planes and loud music – all create tension; this is tiring, as tension involves using muscular energy all the time. There are, of course, pastimes which can put us mentally and physically at ease, such as taking a warm bath, going for a walk by the sea, having a drink with friends, swimming or dancing and, very effectively, being in any situation that makes us laugh. However, actors need to know how to achieve a state of relaxation as a pre-work routine that will help them to function with maximum efficiency. The relaxation exercises that follow are for that purpose.

1

Stand with the feet twelve to eighteen inches apart and reach upwards with fingertips, palms facing and fingers splayed, trying to touch the ceiling. Imagine that there is a wire attached to each fingertip and also one to the crown of the head and that you are being drawn up on to your toes towards the ceiling by the pull of the wires. Feel the body elongate. Try to hold this position for up to a minute; then imagine that the wires are suddenly cut and the hands, wrists, arms, head and shoulders drop and relax after the sustained tension of stretching. Let the arms hang loosely at the sides and the head hang down with the jaw loose. Notice how easy and comfortable the muscles feel after the release of tension. Allow the head and arms to hang for a moment, then adopt an easy, erect posture.

2

Stand as in exercise 1, but thrust rhythmically at the ceiling with the splayed fingertips and the crown of the head. After about five thrusts, hold the position and strain upwards for a silent count of ten. Then let the whole body above the waist relax and slump forward, so that the trunk, arms, hands and head are hanging down in a relaxed, easy manner. Allow the arms to dangle and swing loosely until they come to a halt of their own accord. Hang limply for a few moments and adjust the legs, if you wish, for a better balance.

3

Stand with the feet twelve to eighteen inches apart, with the weight mainly on the balls of the feet. Lightly touch the shoulders with the fingertips, at the same time thrusting out the lower jaw and bending the head back so that you can feel the muscles of the throat stretching. Hold this position for a moment, then let the head slump loosely forward and down with the jaw now loose and the hands and arms swinging freely until they come to rest of their own accord.

4

Stand with the feet apart, thrust the lower jaw out, reach up with the chin and lightly touch the shoulders with the fingertips. Hold this position of tension for a mental count of ten, then let the arms, head and trunk slump forward loosely and relaxed with the arms dangling in front of the legs. Hang down until the arms cease swinging and feel free from tension.

5

Stand with an easy and erect posture. Allow the arms to hang loosely from the shoulders. Gently lift the shoulders in an attempt to touch the ears; roll the shoulders back, let them drop loosely, push them forward, lift them again and so rotate the shoulders in large circles. Do not allow the head to poke forwards as the shoulders roll backwards. Feel the muscles being stretched and loosened.

6

Stand erect, but easily, with feet apart and arms and hands hanging loosely at your sides. Allow the head to drop forward and hang down quite limply, with the jaw loose. Gently swing the head from side to side and feel that the muscles of the neck and throat are becoming easy and relaxed and the head is becoming heavier and freer. After swinging the head from side to side a few times, allow the head to roll completely round; left, drop back, right, drop forward. Roll the head round one way for a few times, then reverse the direction.

7

Adopt an erect posture with the feet apart. Lightly touch the shoulders with the fingertips. Thrust out the lower jaw, bending back the head, and stretch upwards with the chin. Stretch the muscles of the neck. Hold for a moment, then let head, hands and trunk flop loosely forwards with hands and head hanging limply. After a moment come up to an erect posture, then vigorously shake the loose hands, arms and shoulders away from the body in all directions – sideways, forwards, up and down, as though you are trying to throw them off. After a few moments let the arms and hands hang limply. Notice how relaxed and easy they feel.

8

Adopt an erect posture with the feet apart. Reach up with the crown of the head and the fingertips, trying to touch the ceiling. Now turn the fingers outwards to point to the side walls and reach up to the ceiling with the palms of the hands. Keep the hands at right-angles to the arms, lower the straight arms slowly and attempt to touch the thighs with the fingertips when the arms are lowered. This exercise may be found difficult and cause discomfort at first. The object is to stretch the muscles. When the arms have been lowered as much as possible in this position, relax the tension and shake the hands and arms vigorously.

9

Reach up with the fingertips and the crown of the head. Strain upwards as hard as you can. Hold the upward stretch for a moment, then suddenly relax hands, arms, head, neck and trunk and slump down limply; let the head and arms be quite loose with the arms limp and dangling in front of the legs. Hang downwards in this position for a few moments, then roll the trunk to the left, let it flop backwards, then drop to the right, then drop forward again. Roll the trunk round in a complete circle several times, then reverse the direction.

10

Stretch up with the fingertips and crown of the head towards the ceiling. Strain upwards as hard as you can and hold it for a mental count of ten. Then release the tension suddenly and flop, letting the hands, arms, head and trunk drop forward limply, with the arms dangling loosely from the relaxed shoulders in front of the legs. Let yourself hang limply for a few moments until the hands stop swinging. Repeat three times. Then stand and roll the shoulders up, back, down and forward with the arms hanging limply. Then roll the head round loosely in both directions, checking to see if the neck is relaxed. Finally, shake the hands, arms and shoulders away from the body in all directions.

11

Adopt an easy but erect posture. Stretch up with the fingertips and the crown of the head towards the ceiling. Strain upwards as hard as you can and hold it for a mental count of fifteen. Then gradually release the tension, starting with the highest limbs – so that the fingers, hand, wrists, forearms, head, neck, trunk and finally legs relax completely and you crumple softly on to the floor with a smooth controlled movement and lie there inert. This is best done on a carpet. Collapse on one side, as in a stage fall, and roll on to your back. Don't try to hold yourself still, but get comfortable and feel the entire body becoming soft and limp. Try to go to sleep for a moment.

12

Repeat the procedure as in exercise 11, but, when you are completely relaxed after lying prone for a while, stretch outwards with the toes, fingertips, and the crown of the head in a spreadeagled position for a mental count of fifteen – then slump. When stretching, it helps to imagine that the body is being stretched on a rack.

13

Repeat as for exercise 11, but, when you are relaxed and have been lying prone for a minute or so, attempt to arch the body by raising the seat from the floor as high as you can, with the weight being borne by the heels and shoulders.

14

The entire group of students stand in a circle with outstretched arms, holding the shoulders of the people on either side of them for support. Everyone puts their weight on the left leg, leaving the right leg hanging free. Keeping in time, everyone swings the right leg into and out of the circle, swinging the leg higher and higher each time. After about a dozen swings, allow the legs to come to rest of their own accord and hang loosely. When all legs are at rest everyone vigorously tries to shake off the right foot, then the foot and the leg below the knee and finally the entire leg from the hip. Allow the leg to come to rest. Pause for a moment, then place the weight on the now relaxed right leg. Repeat the routine for the left leg. Apart from relaxing the legs and feet, this exercise usually promotes a lot of laughter which is, in itself, relaxing.

15

Students pair up and student A gently manipulates the shoulders, neck and facial muscles of student B with the fingertips for two or three minutes; they then change roles. This is invariably found to be most relaxing. It helps if the person being relaxed can sit on a chair.

2

Posture

When the body has been relaxed, it is important to check that
the posture is such that it will allow the free and expressive use
of voice, speech and movement. These three things are the
physical means whereby the actor transmits to his or her fellow
actors and the audience the thoughts and feelings he or she has
created. Naturally, when characterizing, an actor may use voice,
speech and movement in a manner that differs from what could
be regarded as the optimum use of these faculties – because the
character demands that he or she reveals someone with certain
limitations. However, the revelation of limitations requires the
knowledge of correct usage.

It is surprising how much a person's voice, speech and
movement appear to reveal about his or her state of mind and
personality at the time of observation. The actor in performance
is creating a continuous series of images by his or her movement,
which is conditioned by the posture of the body within which he
or she works.

The posture should not only allow the free and expressive use
of gesture and general movement, but should be conducive to
breathing for voice production with a full range of resonance
and projection of voice and speech. The thorax, larynx,
pharynx, oral and nasal cavities, together with the organs of
articulation, are dependent for their optimum use on the posture
of the actor's body. Common faults that can be observed are:
shoulders rounded, inhibiting easy inhalation; head poked
forwards, distorting the larynx and pharynx, impairing tone;

chin raised too high, leading to tensions in the larynx and pharynx, raising the pitch of voice and limiting vocal range; a hollowed spine in the lumbar region, affecting the balance of the body; weight too much on the heels, which will inhibit fluid movement and possibly upset the alignment of the body for breathing purposes; abdominal muscles slack, leading to poor breath control; a tense military posture, with chest pushed forwards and head held unnaturally high, inhibiting resonance and limiting the use of the voice.

The following exercises should help to develop a poised use of the body, allowing free movement and development of capacity and control of breathing.

1

When relaxed, stand as tall as possible, but in an easy and poised manner, with the weight of the body supported mainly on the balls of the feet and the heels touching the ground for balance. Let the shoulders and arms be loose and comfortable; check that the shoulders are not raised or forced back in a military manner.

2

Stand poised, as for exercise 1, but with the feet apart. Reach out sideways with the hands as far as you can stretch. Splay the fingers, palms to the ground, thumbs pointing forwards. Now turn the palms upwards so that the thumbs are pointing to the rear. Feel the shoulders rolled back as you twist the hands round as far as you can. Continue to stretch outwards for a moment, then very slowly lower the straightened arms and try to touch the thighs with the backs of the fingers. It is not usually possible to get as far as that, but feel the lower part of the chest expand as the arms lower. Do not poke the head forward. This is a good corrective for rounded shoulders.

3

Stand as tall as possible, but be poised and relaxed, with the heels together. Swing the arms forwards, up, sideways and down. As the arms are stretched sideways, twist the hands so that the palms are up and thumbs are to the rear and, as the arms are lowering, bob down by bending the knees, but keep the trunk straight and erect. Swing fast and rhythmically. As you bob down, feel the pelvis thrusting forwards and the spine straightening.

4

Standing with the heels a few inches away from the wall, rest the back against the wall. Allow the arms to hang loosely. Feel that the head is poised, with the chin level. Now bend the knees and allow the body to lower itself. Feel the spinal area in the lumbar region straighten and contact the wall. Slide up and down the wall a few times, feeling the spine straightening as you lower the body.

5

Lie on the floor with something like a rolled-up pullover under the head. Draw your knees up, with the soles of the feet flat on the ground and about twelve inches apart. Allow the arms to rest loosely away from the sides of the body. Feel the back spreading itself out on the floor. Now very slowly draw the knees up in the direction of the chin. This should ensure the straightening of the lumbar area of the spine. Slowly lower the feet to the ground without allowing the back to hollow too much.

6

Stand with your feet about eighteen inches apart. Let the arms hang loosely by the sides. Look your own height and keep the chin level. Feel that the head is poised on top of the spinal column. Gently bounce up and down on the balls of the feet, as though you are poised to move off in any direction. Reach up with the crown of the head on each upward movement, feeling yourself elongating. After about a dozen bounces, come to rest with the weight mainly on the balls of the feet. Make sure your seat is tucked in. Now, holding yourself poised and tall, very gently sway the body forwards and backwards slightly a few times until you have discovered the position at which you feel poised and easy. Stand like that for a moment and remember how it feels to be poised, then move swiftly and easily around the studio, eventually coming to rest with a sense of equilibrium.

3

Breathing and Voice

Good breathing is a fundamental requirement for voice production and also for projecting the actor's speech. By voice is meant the general vocal tone created by the note from the vibrating vocal cords being resonated in the cavities of the pharynx, mouth, nose, sinuses and the chest; speech is a wider term of reference including all speech sounds without special regard to the quality of resonance. It is possible for an actor to speak with a very sonorous and pleasing vocal tone that is redolent of great emotion, and convince us that he is happy or sad or weary or angry. Yet his articulation may not be crisp enough to allow the meaning of what he is saying to emerge because, while the tone of voice used has conveyed general emotion, the articulation has been overwhelmed by the resonance of the voice. Conversely, another actor might deliver a dramatic speech which is excellently timed and shows great clarity of articulation, but fails to move us because the feeling behind the speech is not conveyed by the tone of voice. The actor has to use voice and speech so that both the vocal tone and the articulation work in harmony, with the voice being capable of variety of tone and the speech always audible within that tone.

The breath expelled from the lungs is the force used to create speech sound. Therefore, the air capacity of the chest must be sufficient to allow a steady outflow of breath to sustain long phrases with ease. A plentiful supply of breath also helps to give a sense of confidence. Also, enlarging the chest cavity improves its function as an auxiliary resonator for the voice. It will be felt to vibrate if the hand is placed on the breast bone when a deeper pitch is used; the pharynx is also improved as a resonator by deeper breathing as the larynx is pulled down slightly, enlarging the capacity of the pharynx.

The ability to produce a firm note throughout the range of the voice is essential to maintain vocal quality, and this is controlled largely by a steady breath stream meeting the vocal cords. Attack is the term used to describe the production of the initial note. Thus attack can be too fierce, giving a strident quality to the voice, or too casual, with a resultant breathy or husky quality.

It is also essential to ensure that the voice is being used within its natural range and that the centre note used is neither too high nor too low for the compass of the voice. Habitual tension in the larynx and body usually raises the voice to an uncomfortably strained high pitch, so that the true voice is rarely heard.

The requirements for good voice production are relaxation, good posture, a plentiful supply of breath, controlled use of breathing by diaphragm and intercostal muscles, relaxed and unconstricted oral and pharyngeal resonators, and the formation of sounds well forward in the mouth to avoid throaty tone and to assist projection. Attention should be diverted from the larynx itself as it normally operates satisfactorily when the above conditions prevail. Thinking about the larynx induces throaty tone.

This is a very instructive, although uncomfortable, exercise to demonstrate how breathing affects vocal tone, projection and clarity of speech. The tutor takes a good breath and starts counting aloud for as long as possible without replenishing the breath. It will be observed that the initially resonant tone degenerates to a harsh rasp, projection becomes more and more difficult and articulation becomes inaudible.

1

Lie comfortably on the floor. Allow the arms to rest about six inches away from the body, with the hands loose. Draw the knees up until the soles of the feet are flat on the floor and you feel that the back is resting its length on the floor without a gap in the lumbar region. Lie there for a few moments feeling the back spreading wide, then place the hands gently on the lower side ribs. Breathe slowly in through the nose and out through the mouth, becoming aware of the movement of the thorax as you inhale and exhale. As you inhale, the lower side ribs will expand and the diaphragm will descend, as you exhale the lower side ribs will go in and the diaphragm will rise. Now try panting like a dog – in and out rapidly – to become aware of the power you can exert over your breath when you wish. Next breathe in gently through the nose to a count of five, hold the breath for a moment and then allow it to flow out silently from a wide open jaw for a count of five. All the movement must be in the lower part of the chest. Do not be tempted to take in too much air at any one time or it will lead to tension.

2

Lying on the floor after relaxation exercises is a good way to begin breathing routines, but an actor does most of his or her talking while standing or sitting, so for this exercise stand easy and erect with the feet apart, rest the backs of the hands on the lower side ribs, making sure that the shoulders are loose and not raised. Breathe in, noiselessly, to a mental count of one-two-three. Feel the outward swing of the lower ribs pushing the hands out. Release the breath gently to a mental count of one–two–three. Take in only sufficient air to enable you to feel the ribs swing out. On no account raise the shoulders; confine the movement to the lower ribs. Repeat this twelve times.

3

Adopt an easy and erect posture. Rest the backs of the hands on
the lower side ribs, with arms propped out loosely and shoulders
relaxed. To a mental count of one–two–three gently inhale
through the nose and feel the lower ribs swing out. Do not inhale
too much air. Let the lower jaw drop open (tongue flat, tip
behind lower teeth) and gently exhale the air from the mouth to
a mental count of one–two–three. Feel the warm air flowing out
through the open mouth. Remember the rhythmical sequence:
inhale through the nose and lower ribs move out; let jaw drop
open; exhale slowly. Next, increase the inhalation and exhalation
by one mental count each time, until a capacity of ten has been
reached. Repeat this six times.

4

Rest the backs of the hands on the lower side ribs. Inhale silently
through the nose to a mental count of one–two–three–four–five.
Drop the jaw wide open, round and push the lips forward as for
the sound 'oo', remembering to keep the jaw open. Now blow
five short firm breaths from the rounded lips to a target on the
other side of the studio. Feel that the force of the outgoing
breath is capable of being heard at the target area. Repeat the
sequence six times.

5

Standing poised as before, with the backs of the hands resting on
the lower side ribs, inhale silently through the nose to a mental
count of one–two–three–four–five–six. Do not inflate the chest
too much. Aiming at a target on the other side of the studio, say

aloud, 'one–two–three,' with open jaw and active articulation. Don't use all the breath, let the rest sigh out. Repeat the sequence six times.

6

Adopt an easy, erect posture with feet apart. Rest the back of one hand on the lower side ribs and the fingers of the other on the area of the abdominal muscles, between the end of the breast bone and the navel. Inhale quietly through the nose. You will feel one hand being pushed out by the movement of the side ribs, and the fingers of the other pushed out as the abdominal muscles relax – to allow room for the diaphragm to lower as the thoracic cavity is enlarged at its base. Exhale quietly. You will feel the ribs descend and the abdominal muscles contract as the diaphragm rises while air is expelled from the lungs. Now drop the jaw wide open and pant in and out like a dog, and feel the movements of the rib cage and the diaphragm working rhythmically together. Next, select your target on the other side of the studio, take a quick breath by the mouth and, using an open jaw and lively articulation, throw the sounds 'one-two-three-four-five' to the target, feeling that the breath and the numbers you project are a single factor of communication – the breath is the projected sound.

7

Stand poised. Let the arms hang relaxed by your sides. Breathe in and out with your own natural breathing rhythm a few times. Feel how your breathing capacity has increased and how you now have control over the way in which you can project it. Now, inhaling swiftly and silently through the open jaw, using lively articulation and projecting the sounds to your target across the studio, say aloud, 'one,' inhale, 'one–two,' inhale, 'one–two–three,' and so on up to ten or fifteen, or whatever your lung capacity will allow without feeling any strain. Next, repeat the routine, but varying the volume, pace and pitch. See how much animation you can bring to just a series of numbers. Try saying them in different ways – angrily, happily, doubtfully, confidentially, for example. Now move about the studio filling the space with your sounds. Let the movement of your body and the sounds you create be as one – as a single act of communication.

4

Warming–up Exercises

Before a group of student actors can begin working together truly creatively a process has to be gone through that is usually referred to as warming-up. By this is meant not only being relaxed and having the body and imagination in good shape, but also having a sense of group awareness, cooperation, mental and physical accord, a feeling of camaraderie and a lack of inhibitions. Most professional actors, aided by their training and conscious of limited rehearsal time, quickly acquire the ability to develop these attitudes during rehearsals, so that by the time of the first night there is a feeling of ensemble, although it may take a few weeks of audience contact for a play to be 'run in'.

When starting to work with students on such an exposing experience as improvisation, members of groups naturally feel vulnerable, because they don't know one another and they have no idea how the others think, speak, move, or respond, mentally and physically. Moreover, they don't know how they themselves will react in these challenging circumstances. For the inexperienced it can be a somewhat daunting prospect. It is therefore invaluable to preface improvisation and even rehearsals with a warming-up session to remove certain inhibitions and taboos.

The strongest fear is that of making a fool of oneself, revealing inadequacies or 'failing' in one's task. Another worry is that of making physical contact with other people. Anglo-Saxons, in particular, tend to be fairly repressed and non-tactile people. This limits the degree to which some people feel free to demonstrate relationships physically.

The warming-up exercises are designed in the form of games in which corporate physical activity is the aim. This means that performers are automatically absolved from the need to 'win' or expose themselves to criticism. Further, as most of the warming-up exercises are group activities, the individual's allegiance is to working with and responding to his or her group, thus gaining security and anonymity. It is almost equivalent to wearing a mask, behind which the imagination can operate with a sense of fantasy and freedom that is sometimes dampened when an inexperienced performer feels he or she is the sole focus of attention. The dynamics of group activity are liberating for the imagination and also develop an acute group awareness, so that after a time it often becomes apparent that a group is thinking and reacting as an entity. Some sort of sixth sense seems to emerge that informs the group of the mood and motivations of its individual members, so that split-second adjustments in attitudes can be adapted to the group task. A group empathy develops.

The warming-up exercises allow students to react, freed from unnecessary mental and physical tensions, within a series of vigorous situations. They make it possible for group awareness to develop, accompanied by a growing confidence of the participants in themselves as performers willing to plunge imaginatively into improvised drama.

SHAPES

This exercise calls for instant reaction from the entire group to an order from the tutor telling them to form a shape. They must act as one unit, but nobody should speak, although members of the group may physically guide others to complete the required shape quickly. The exercise usually provokes laughter. The tutor only gives the order once so that the group must listen and then move swiftly and silently into the shape. As soon as one shape is completed, the tutor gives the order for the next shape and so on. Speed, discipline and economy of movement are required.

Some examples are:

Square	□
Equals sign	=
Multiplication sign	✕
Question mark	?
Square-root sign	√
Exclamation mark	!
Division sign	÷
Circle	○
The letter Z	Z
The number 4	4
Triangle	△
Straight line	—

RED, BLUE, YELLOW

Each member of the group gets a chair swiftly, and sits in a circle with a space between each chair. (You need strong chairs for this exercise.) The tutor quickly gives each person in the circle a colour, alternating between red and blue. The tutor must explain that the purpose of the exercise is precise movement, with no fuss and in complete silence. On the order 'Red!', all the Reds must rise and find another chair. On the order 'Blue!', all the Blues have to find another chair. On the order 'Yellow!', everyone finds another chair. Vary the manner in which the movement is to be carried out – from lightning reaction to slow motion. No contact may be made and the transfer from one chair to another must be made with the minimum of movement. Start giving the orders slowly and then speed up to get very quick reactions. People usually start laughing as the exercise speeds up; this shows that people are relaxed and have a group awareness.

THE MIRROR EXERCISE

This is an elaboration of an old exercise. The purpose is to encourage observation, quick reaction, inventiveness and projection of image and sound. You need a group of at least eight people. Divide the group into two lines, everyone sitting on spaced-out chairs facing a partner. Call one line A and the other line B. The two lines should be about twelve feet apart. During the exercise the chairs are static, but the performers are not. There are three stages to the exercise: first, second and third.

First

When the tutor calls 'A!' all the members of line A jump up from their chairs and put their bodies into any position they choose and hold that position. Each person in line B mentally photographs the posture of the partner opposite. On the order 'B!' all the members of line B jump up from their chairs and copy the posture of their partner. Allow both lines to hold their postures for a few seconds. The tutor then calls 'C!' and lines A and B relax their postures and move one place, clockwise, to the next chair. The people at the ends of the rows have to race across to the opposite line. If the group has an odd number there can be a chair for the odd one out at one end of the two lines. When the routine is established you may speed up the process until you are getting very quick reactions and change-overs.

Second

The routine is the same as above, but, instead of a bodily posture that is held absolutely still, on the order 'A!' everyone in line A makes a continual pattern of movement with their bodies. Line B observes this movement pattern for a moment and when the tutor calls 'B!' line B copy the movement pattern until the order 'C!' is given and all move clockwise by one place.

Third

Here a further complication is added. Each person moving must invent a sound of some sort to accompany their particular movement. This usually gets hilarious and noisy, so the tutor will have to call 'B!' and 'C!' very loudly if there is a large group. If there are two lines of ten people, people in line B will have to listen intently to pick out their partner's sound from the other nine being projected simultaneously.

With the above exercise the pace may be varied from fast to slow motion and the movements from emphatic to very subtle. If lines A and B are placed further apart the degree of concentration demanded will be greater.

MIRROR PAIRS

First

The aim is the same as for the previous exercise, but the routine is different. One person is A and the other B. They work about ten feet from each other. A starts off by striking a posture. B copies it and holds it for a few seconds, then both relax. A then repeats the first posture, relaxes it and immediately adds another and relaxes it. B copies the first and second postures. A then repeats the first and second postures and adds a third posture. B copies these. This sequence continues until A has presented six postures and B has copied them faithfully. Roles are then changed and B in turn presents a series of postures to be copied by A.

Second

The same as above, but instead of posture there is a continuous movement of some kind.

Third

The same as above, but the continuous movement is accompanied by sounds to be projected to the partner.

COMPLEMENTARY SHAPES

This is an exercise for groups of six or more people, in which each person has to relate to the rest of the group with his or her entire mental attitude, reflecting a theme set by the tutor. The theme, which can be a mood or happening, is suggested by a word or phrase. The exercise helps students to understand the use of stage grouping and imagery in dramatic communication. It also fosters a feeling of ensemble and helps to break down inhibitions about physical contact. In the beginning it is wise to ask the group to carry out the routine slowly, as a dummy run, so that they have time to absorb the idea.

The tutor's instructions might go something like this: 'Please sit back, spaced evenly around the walls of the studio. I want one volunteer to come to the centre and put his or her body into any shape they like. Make sure it's not too awkward to hold for a few minutes. Thank you. Now everyone else look at that shape in the centre – it's part of a design within this space. I want you to visualize how you can, one by one, come out and position yourself to complement or build up what that shape suggests. You can either link up physically, or be at a distance, as long as what you do relates to the whole.'

Slowly, one by one, people move to the centre and build up a sculptural shape. It is extraordinary how impressive some of the human groupings can be. When the procedure is understood the exercise can work with great speed.

Here are some examples of themes that might be suggested:

Celebration
Nightmare
Explosion
Monster
Picnic
Shipwreck
Ambush
Famine
Circus
Grand opera
Roman fountain
Shame
Victory parade
Conspiracy
Orgy
Freezing
Terror
Silence
War memorial
Execution

When the group have built up an interesting sculptural shape, tell them to hold it for a moment and ask them to turn their heads to see how each individual has contributed to the total image.

CATCH ON

The whole group, including the tutor, sit in a circle. The object of the exercise is to stimulate quick responses. The idea is to start off an idea that is taken round the circle as fast as possible. You can begin by simply numbering round the circle until you come to the tutor. The tutor can carry on numbering round, but increasing the speed, or he or she can change to another tack, such as months of the year, the alphabet, associated words, pairs of things, rhymes, a story to which each person contributes a sentence, or the countries of the world. Another alternative is a word list in which the tutor gives a word, the second person repeats that word and adds his or her own, the third person repeats the first and second words and then adds his or her own, and so on until the last person has a whole string of words to put before his or her own.

As soon as an idea begins to flag, start a new one to keep up the momentum of quick reactions.

INITIATIVE

This exercise can either be acted silently or with spontaneous dialogue. Get the group to sit around the studio walls. Let them know that you will want each one in turn to come into the centre of the acting area and start some sort of action for which they will need the help of the rest of the group. Give them up to five minutes to plan something, with, perhaps, a reserve idea in case someone else uses their first choice. When the preparation time is up, call the name of the first person. It might work like this:

A rushes into the acting area, sees an imaginary blaze, yells to the others, 'Help! Fire!' and then fills an imaginary bucket with water. He or she then throws it over the flames as all the others come to the rescue with water buckets, hoses or fire blankets. The scene may build up into a hugh conflagration, with some people rescuing trapped inhabitants of the blazing building, salvaging furniture and goods. In a situation like this you would expect a lot of spontaneous dialogue and noise. When the scene has reached a climax and before it loses momentum, the tutor can terminate it with 'Thank you.'

Ideas that might be developed are:

Road accident
Wedding
Funeral
Car break-down
Fruit picking
At the sales
Lost foreigner
Auction
Wallet falls down grating

PUSH IN

This scene for three people demands continual concentration and determination by all the participants. It is often quite noisy and usually very amusing to watch. Ask the students to divide into groups of three and to decide who is going to be A, B and C. When this has been decided, C leaves the group, so that A and B can plan what they are going to do or discuss without C knowing. C has to think of some impending disaster that can only be avoided if A and B stop their activity and help C. The task of A and B is to pursue their activity with absolute concentration, ignoring C, who is determined to get the full attention and assistance of A and B.

With the rest of the group as an audience, A and B start their activity in the acting area. C then enters the area determined to get their full attention. The situation develops into a battle of concentration; A and B completely ignore C who may do almost anything, within reason, to attract their attention. Similarly, A and B may resort to a variety of ploys to pretend C doesn't exist. Stop the exercise before A, B and C are exhausted.

HELP!

This is related to the previous exercise as its aim is to encourage complete concentration on a task. It works with groups of four. There is no need for an audience, as all groups can work simultaneously. The four are called A, B, C and D. They must each remember who the other three are because:

B urgently needs assistance from A

C urgently needs assistance from B

D urgently needs assistance from C

A urgently needs assistance from D

The idea is that each of the four participants will be trying desperately to get assistance from a fellow group member, while simultaneously being pestered for something. The aim is to persist in their request while refusing to be distracted by a requester. Any ploy may be tried to gain attention. This is a very lively, noisy and exhausting exercise. Stop it before it flags.

BUZZ-BUZZ

This warming-up exercise, like the MIRROR exercises on pages 36–8, encourages observation, inventiveness, freedom of physical expression and the feeling of ensemble.

In this exercise, the whole group are jogging about in the studio space. The tutor has a buzzer or something that makes a strident noise. When the buzzer sounds, everyone freezes and looks at a 'victim' at whom the tutor points. The tutor buzzes again and the 'victim' instantly acquires his own extraordinary movement routine and leaps into action. Immediately all the group are affected in the same way. The action continues for, say, ten seconds, then the tutor buzzes again, everyone freezes and the tutor points to another 'victim'. Stop the exercise before people start to flag.

PHYSICAL GUIDING

This is a contact and confidence exercise. Arrange the studio chairs along one wall of the studio in a jumbled shape, like an elongated maze. Allow room for people to walk through the maze without having to touch a chair or the wall, and stipulate that people moving in this maze must not stray into the clear area beyond. The group must be informed that the chairs forming the maze are electrified as is the area outside the maze. Students work in pairs, A and B.

A is blind, so he or she must keep his or her eyes closed or be blindfolded. B, who is dumb, physically guides the blind A through the maze without either of them getting electrocuted. Pairs follow one another through the maze, ensuring that there is sufficient space between them to avoid collision. As people come out of the maze they quietly sit and watch others working their way through. In discussions after the exercise A people frequently state that they experienced a feeling of trust and dependence upon their B partners, while B people felt a sense of responsibility and a strong awareness of the importance of precise movement. Both groups felt that the exercise consolidated the feeling of a group entity.

ORAL GUIDING

This is an extension of the previous exercise. The maze is used in a similar way, but B is now blind, while A can see and speak but has no arms. The task of A is to guide the blind B through the electrified area by very precise spoken instructions. Any vagueness or lack of exactitude on the part of A may lead to B's electrocution. For this reason B must listen to A and do exactly what A says. Group reactions to the exercise are similar to those for PHYSICAL GUIDING. In addition, the exercise helps the group to become aware of the importance of precise and clearly articulated instructions.

MASS ACTING TO NARRATION

This is a useful exercise for students who, at an early stage, are diffident about performing before an audience. Here the group is performing *en masse*, the ideas are supplied by the tutor, and if desired the lights may be dimmed to help concentration on the visualization of the story. To begin the exercise, the tutor should ask each student to find his or her own space on the floor and to sit with eyes closed in order to visualize what the tutor is about to narrate. When they have visualized the circumstances and it is time for them to get involved, they should open their eyes, move away and act out the situation in which they are the central character. No dialogue is needed. Here is a typical idea:

'You are on holiday abroad. You are sitting in your chair at a café table in some Mediterranean resort on a hot day. The waiter brings you the menu. You can't speak the language, so you point to what you hope is a long, cold drink. The waiter goes. To pass the time you check that your camera, passport and loose change are all right. The waiter comes back with a drink in a tall glass with a long spoon. You dip the spoon in the drink and find some delicious bits of ice-cold fruit – which you eat. Suddenly a tall man, dressed in long robes with carpets over his arm, comes up to your table to try to sell you a carpet. He waves them in front of you. Bits of fluff drop into your drink. You wave him angrily away. He swears at you and spits on the ground next to your feet . . .'

The tutor can continue to describe how they pay the bill, explore the back streets, have their camera stolen, etc.

Many commonplace incidents give opportunity for visualizing and reacting in terms of movement.

Some ideas are:

Posting a letter in dense fog

Exploring an old deserted house

Walking in difficult terrain – deep mud, on ice, boulders, snow, in the dark, in thick undergrowth, through floods

Being involved in a tightrope-walking act

Waking up very late – washing, dressing, snatching a bite to eat, hurrying for the train

It may be wise not to have an inquest on basic movement exercises like this if the object is simply to stimulate movement and reaction, but just to let the group savour the experience. There will be many occasions later when the tutor can analyse work performed.

Acting Without Dialogue

This section is called 'Acting Without Dialogue' rather than 'Mime', because mime, as a performing art in its own right, demands a movement approach that is more emphatic and stylized than one normally encounters in drama. Therefore the aim in this section is to strive for clarity of communication without speech by using graphic, but less stylized, movement.

Without dialogue, movement must be explicit and very carefully timed in order to communicate. An initial fault is too casual, swift or vague use of movement. In order to concentrate the performer's mind on what his or her movement is trying to 'say' to the observers, and to space out the various movement 'statements', it is sometimes an interesting experiment to ask students working solo to describe to themselves, aloud, what they are doing, why they are doing it and how they are doing it. Here is an example:

'Home at last! I feel exhausted. Can't wait to fall into bed. Key? Which pocket's the damned key in? In here? No. In there? No. Here? Fumble – fumble – Ah! Got it! Careful! Don't drop it. Bloody dark, can't see the keyhole. Feel with fingers. Yes – there! Won't turn. Ah! Wrong key. This one. It goes in, but won't turn! What? Ah! Wrong door.'

A routine like this helps to make students aware that the commonplace movements we make automatically must be timed and clarified in order to communicate them to an audience.

I believe that a healthy and relaxed performer transmits some kind of signal that informs the audience of his or her presence and mood. The phenomenon is clearly observed in some performers; it is a kind of personal magnetism that illuminates their work. It is dependant upon imagination, vitality, concentration and complete confidence. It is diminished by fatigue or ill health. Metaphorically speaking, some people have the ability to reach out and embrace both the cast and the entire audience. In turn, an audience can transmit back to the cast on the stage the degree of attention and appreciation with which they are responding. Most actors are familiar with the rapport that can be established between audience and cast. Jean-Louis Barrault considers that a human being is surrounded by a magnetic aura, which impinges and transmits an awareness of presence. Stanislavski talked about a process of irradiation that streams out of us at moments of strong emotion. He regarded it as an inner, invisible and spiritual force that he knew existed, but could not explain. Antonin Artaud says, 'The gifted actor finds by instinct how to tap and radiate certain powers.' Peter Brook talks about the function of a language other than words; in this instance, a language of actions.

In acting without dialogue, apart from having a body that is flexible and expressive, a vivid imagination is an essential requirement. The actor should be able to visualize the invisible, to make concrete the intangible and, where appropriate, to call into play the senses of taste, smell and hearing. All the five senses may thus be used to clarify meaning. The reactions to this invisible world in which the actor finds himself must be dramatically truthful and conveyed with a precision of carefully timed movement that tells an audience exactly what is happening at each moment.

The actor should also remember sensory impressions and emotional responses to a wide range of life experiences, so that these may be utilized to give the essential foundation of truth to a performance. Where certain happenings have not been experienced, such as dying, imagination and a sense of creative fantasy will have to be used. In the exercise REMEMBER, where a physical action is carried out, the task is to remember, as truthfully as possible, the muscular stresses, the all-important shape of the grip and the reaction of the rest of the body. The grip, the space within the hand, together with the position of the arm and the rest of the body, make a statement to observers about the item within the grip. The audience should have a clear idea of the weight, bulk, texture and, when incorporated into the exercise, the actor's feelings about the job he or she is doing. Together with transmitting information about what is being done, a complete range of emotions and attitudes may be conveyed. As Stanislavski says in *An Actor Prepares* when discussing emotion memory, external actions will be cold and pointless unless they are motivated by a feeling or attitude generated from within the actor.

The first three exercises are well-tried routines in which the performer is sitting and needs to use only the hands to communicate.

GIFT

The group, including the tutor, is sitting in a circle. Each person is told that they have a present of some kind on their laps or on a table in front of them. The concentration will be on the use of hands showing what the item is and how it is being used. Remind the group that the hands must show the shape, the weight and the texture of the gift. Allow one minute for the idea to be visualized. Then work round the circle one by one, each person picking up and doing something with the item to 'state' what it is, to demonstrate its weight, texture and use. Each person should take only a few seconds and then members of the group, at random, can name the item. If no one gets it right the performer must repeat and refine the 'statement' the hands are making until the correct answer is given.

A JOB OF WORK

The group is sitting as for the previous exercise. This time the task is to visualize a job of work that is done by hand. The hands must clearly 'state' what they are doing. It is important not to blur movements, but to keep them crisp and clear. As soon as someone names the job the next person begins his or her task. If no one comes up with the right answer, the job must be repeated until the correct answer is given.

WHAT IS IT NOW?

The group is sitting as for the last two exercises. Ask them to watch you very carefully as you pick up an imaginary item of a certain shape, weight and texture, handle it for a moment and then pass it to the person next to you. The person receiving it must handle it for a few seconds as if it were the same thing, but then it suddenly changes into something quite different. This new item is then passed on to the third person and, after a few seconds, it changes again – and so on all round the circle.

REMEMBER

The group are sitting on chairs spaced throughout the studio area. The tutor asks them to pick up their chairs with one hand and to move around the studio carrying them. As they move, they must become aware of the exact shape of their hands and of the physical stresses they feel as they hold and move the chairs around. After a couple of circuits of the studio they put down their chairs and sit on them, recalling the shape of the grip they used and the stresses they felt. They then rise from their chairs and pick up an imaginary chair, experiencing the situation with a sense of dramatic truth, because they are visualizing and remembering clearly as they move around the studio. This can be repeated with a whole range of objects.

TABLEAUX

This exercise is to give an understanding of how grouping and gesture facilitate the communication of a stage image. Ask the group to divide into smaller groups of three or four, to sit in a circle well away from other groups, and then to plan a tableau which they are to present. For this, each group picks an incident from, say, literature, history, pantomime, legend, or a topical event, and plans a scene in which the general grouping, as well as the posture and gestures of each person, clearly convey both the incident portrayed and the characters involved. Give the groups five minutes to choose the incident, to cast it, and to decide how their grouping, posture and gesture will make the tableau immediately understood by the rest of the group. Remind them that, as no movement or speech is required, they must all freeze as soon as they get into position. After the presentation of each tableau, the groups acting as an audience can make constructive comments on how something could be clarified.

Here are some ideas:

> King Canute and the tide
> Henry V's speech before Harfleur
> Oliver Twist asking for more
> Goldilocks: 'Who's been eating my porridge?'
> Frankenstein's monster
> 'If music be the food of love, play on!' (*Twelfth Night*)
> The dumb-show from *Hamlet*, where the King has poison put in his ear
> The judgement of Paris
> The Mad Hatter's tea party

These tableaux also help to give students ideas for creating focal points for audience attention, with the use of elevation, triangulation, gesture and cast concentration.

WINDOW DRESSING

Groups of about four people plan a shop window dressing scene in which some of the group are window dressers and some are flexible dummies. The idea is to pick a window dressing display in which the dummies are dressed and positioned so as to make clear what the objects on sale are and whether they represent any particular season or activity.

Allow approximately five minutes for planning. As in the other exercises in this section, there is no dialogue. Therefore the positioning and grouping of the dummies, without any tangible properties or costumes, must make 'statements'; for this reason the use of the hands is very important.

When the window dressers have done their work, they leave the acting area with the dummies on display. The rest of the group, as an audience, then discuss what is being shown and try to establish exactly what it represents.

MOVING IN

This exercise is to encourage visualization and precision of movement. The entire group sit on chairs arranged in a square of about twelve feet square. There is a gap at one corner representing an open door.

The routine is as follows:

The group divide into smaller groups of five or six to plan what item of furniture each will bring in. They may combine to bring in quite heavy things. The contours, size, weight and texture of the article must be made clear as it is brought in. When each small group comes to furnish their room, they leave the square of chairs and position themselves outside the gap representing the door. Each must know the order in which they have to enter and where to place their own item. As each item is placed, the furnisher does something with it to demonstrate what and where it is and then exits through the gap. Each subsequent member of a group must remember exactly where previously placed items are and not walk through them. When all the items have been placed by a group, the tutor elicits from the audience the names and placings of everything and also checks whether any member of the group forgot the position of a previously placed bit of furniture. Each group, of course, starts with an empty room.

WHAT'S THE PRODUCT?

The group divide themselves into teams of four to six people. Each team is manufacturing a product on a moving assembly line in a factory. The team stand in a line, facing the audience. One starts off on the first job and, when finished, puts the product on to the moving assembly line for the second person to pick up and do his or her work on it. The first then starts his or her routine again. The product passes on from person to person, with each starting his or her routine again, so eventually all are working all the time. The last person in the line is the tester who tries the product out and stacks it away. The exercise calls for careful movement and timing. The audience have to discover what each person on the assembly line is doing and what the final product is. If there is any uncertainty, they can ask the assembly line to repeat and clarify the routine.

RITUAL

This is an exercise for developing teamwork, concentration and timing and the creation of a mood by the style of movement. It works well with groups of about six to eight people. The task of the groups is to devise a ritual, or ceremony, based on primitive or contemporary society. The object is to create and sustain an appropriate mood and group relationship through movement. There is no dialogue, but song, chanting, intonation, dance or percussion can be used to build up the atmosphere. Preparation time needs to be generous, with perhaps a rehearsal of the complete routine.

WAITERS

This exercise is designed to encourage economy and precision of movement. The group must work within a restricted area. This can be arranged by defining a zone, say a square, outlined by benches or chairs. The members of the group sit on their own chairs in the corners of the square, with roughly the same number in each corner. The routine is for each person to hold their chair high, with one hand under the seat – as a waiter does with a tray – and carry the chair carefully to another corner, put it down silently, go to another corner, collect a chair someone else has put down and deliver it to another corner and so on. Start the action slowly to get the routine going, then speed it up. Insist on silence and alertness to avoid collisions. Stop before people flag.

WHAT IS IT?

This is an exercise to develop visualization and communication and is related to the TACTILE BOX exercise on page 57.

Ask everyone in the group to think of something that can be brought into the acting area and used or handled in such a way that the audience should be able to understand what it is meant to be. Each person is to act with the item for a few moments and then sit down, leaving the imaginary object on stage. Allow a minute or two for people to visualize what they can bring on and how they can use it.

When all are prepared, pick someone (A) to bring on the first thing. When A sits down, pick someone at random (B) to go into the acting area and 'prove' what the item is supposed to be by acting with it for a few moments. If B does not understand what the object is, A must repeat his or her act with more precision until B understands what the thing is and can also act with it.

WHO IS IT?

This is an exercise to improve visualization, timing and reaction. The group divide into pairs and devise a short scene in which an invisible third character is playing a part. This will call for very careful timing and reaction to the invisible third character. If the visualization is strong, the timing is subtle and reactions are revealing, the audience should be able to say at the end of the scene who, or what type of person, the third character was.

PLEASE DO THIS . . .

Ask the members of the group to think of a simple request they can make to another member of the group, using only movement. Allow a few minutes for people to visualize how they can mime their request. With the group arranged as an audience, pick the first person (A) to take up a position on one side of the acting area and a 'victim' (B) to do so on the other side. A and B then encounter in the centre, where A immediately tries to communicate to B his or her particular request. A will have to persist with his or her mimed request until B understands and complies. Neither can leave the acting area until the request has been fulfilled.

COMBAT

The group divide into pairs. Each pair then prepares a brief fight sequence between the two individuals, in which all movement is in slow motion and no real force is used by the combatants. The exercise will demand co-ordination, action and reaction, and control of movement. It may be a fist fight, sword fight, knife fight or wrestling match. Timing will have to be carefully gauged. Preparation time for an exercise like this needs to be very generous. It is a good idea to have the fights performed simultaneously and then to pick a few for performance to the rest of the group for the purpose of discussion.

INCIDENT

In dramatic performance, points are sometimes blurred by indeterminate movement. This exercise is to demonstrate to students how the significance of a dramatic moment can be clarified by means of posture and gesture.

The tutor gives the students three minutes to imagine an incident which they are to portray in three separate postures, each of which is to be held for a few seconds.

The three stages are:

Before it happens
As it is happening
After it has happened

After each incident is shown, the rest of the group can comment or ask the performer to repeat it to clarify the significance of posture and gesture.

MOODS

The members of the group are given time to visualize a simple action that they can carry out in the acting area. This is to be carried out three times, but each performance of the action has to convey a completely different mood. The moods should be substantiated by a concrete reason for being in that mood, and this should be expressed through timing, posture and gesture. The tutor should advise the members of the group to take their time and not to go into the action until they are fully prepared. After each set of three actions, the audience should attempt to name the moods.

LOOK AT IT

The tutor asks the members of the group to think of something, animate or inanimate, which they can come and look at within the acting area. They may not touch it or act with it, but just look at it and react to it. When acting without dialogue it is usually difficult to be specific. However, it is quite surprising how much can often be communicated by subtle reactions of the face, eyes and the rest of the physique. No one should attempt to start the exercise until they feel fully prepared and able to visualize the object very clearly. The performer must be relaxed to enable the audience to 'read' his or her subtle reactions. After each visualization, the audience can volunteer opinions as to what they thought the object of attention was.

TACTILE BOX

This is an exercise for tactile recognition and communication. The tutor will need a cardboard box with flaps, about twelve inches square, and put inside it as many small commonplace articles as there are members of the group. The contents should be things like a key, a candle, a clothes peg, a pencil, etc., and there should be only one of each in the box. The flaps of the box must be together allowing a hand to be slipped inside, but no one may see the contents. Place the box in the centre of the acting area. The task is for people, one by one, to come out and kneel on the far side of the box facing the audience, who check that the performer does not look inside while putting a hand into the box and identifying one article by touch. The performer then withdraws his or her hand, leaving the article in the box, and mimes an action making use of it. The audience then call out what the article is. If they don't guess right, the performer must repeat the action. Subsequent performers have to remember what articles have already been mimed and avoid them, so the last person may have to identify a host of things before the unmimed article is found.

TRANSFORMATION

This can be a solo or group exercise. The performers are told that, in the acting area, there is a collection of all kinds of period costume, or sporting or working apparel, that they choose to imagine.

They are given about three minutes to select what sort of outfit they are going to wear and to decide how the wearing of that outfit will transform them into different sorts of people because, as they put on these garments, they will gradually acquire the characteristics suggested by the clothing. The students will therefore enter the acting area as themselves, start the transformation as they are dressing, and then leave with a new movement pattern and attitude.

The audience should be able to describe how people are dressed and how the movement and attitude have changed.

WHERE'S THE PAIN?

The group sit in a circle. The tutor asks them to sit very comfortably and then to imagine that a severe pain is developing in some part of their body. No sound may be made, neither may the painful area be touched but, as the pain grows, the body may be allowed to adjust itself, reflecting the discomfort and tension caused by the pain. Allowing a few minutes for people's imaginations to get to work, the tutor then concentrates on each person in the circle in turn and attempts to sense where the 'pain' is located. If the performers are imagining strongly and the entire physique has reacted, it is surprising how clearly the general area of the pain can be communicated by the majority of performers.

SENSATIONS

This can operate either by solo performers communicating to the rest of the group as an audience, or as a whole group exercise in which the performers *en masse* are transmitting their sensations to the tutor. The strong function of any one of the five senses, in an expressive person, usually triggers the body to respond also. For example, a very unpleasant taste in the mouth will not only be sensed by the organs of taste, but the revulsion will be reflected by the physique as a whole – in this case mainly by the face and hands. It is important to remember that any physical adjustment must be triggered by a dramatically

truthful stimulus or the sensation portrayed will appear false.
Some ideas are:

Taste: bitterness; hot curry; rancid butter; sweetness
Smell: perfume; gas leak; mountain air; choking smoke
Touch: a caress; a blow; a snake; an ice block
Sight: a prizefight; sunrise; an accident; bank statement
Hearing: scandal; a bore; gunfire; a compliment

SILENCE

This exercise demands teamwork, self-discipline and concentration. The basic information the group is given to work on is
that they are in an environment where absolute silence is
imperative; any sound will be disastrous.

In the planning period the group will have to decide:

Where they are
What they are doing there
Who each character is
What occurs, at the end, when there is a noise

The mode of communication between the actors will have to
be very carefully planned and the movement will need careful
co-ordination. Although the scene may be fairly brief, generous
preparation time should be allowed.

6

Dramatic Situations for Group Improvisation

The use of improvisation in training the actor is to stimulate the dramatic imagination, encourage spontaneity, quick reactions, give and take of ideas, development of character, character interaction, animated dialogue, movement skills and a feeling of ensemble. It offers the opportunity to savour short, complete dramatic situations in which students can acquire technique without having to interpret a formal text.

Improvisation, as a training discipline, allows the actor to discover how the impulse that drives a character finds its expression in spontaneous dramatic movement and dialogue realized in terms of his or her own interpretation. Awareness of developing technique leads to the acquisition of one of the actor's basic requirements, confidence, for the actor knows that he or she can create, develop and control a dramatic situation.

Improvisation is sometimes used by directors as a way of introducing the themes of a play to a cast. Methods vary very much indeed. In the occasional departure from a rehearsal schedule, a particular passage can be clarified by improvising around related themes; John Fernald finds this helpful when the actual words of the text seem to create a barrier to their proper realization. Joan Littlewood often withheld the text until the themes, characters, situations and atmosphere had been created by improvising around carefully devised situations. Littlewood's *Oh What a Lovely War*, as first performed at the Theatre Royal, Stratford, London, was given its final shape by improvisation.

Mike Leigh creates entire plays by means of improvisation. These have been very successful indeed, notably *Abigail's Party* which was seen on television. Keith Johnstone, formerly of the Royal Court Theatre, founded a company of performers, called the Theatre Machine, who give a full evening's entertainment based on improvisational ideas, some of which are thrown at them by the audience. In the past, Meyerhold and Stanislavski found improvisation invaluable. Contemporary directors Peter Brook, Harold Clurman, Clifford Williams and Jonathan Miller, among others, use improvisation when it is felt that it is the best way to solve a problem. However, pressure of rehearsal time does not always allow a director to use improvisation in this way. There are those who think that working on the text is the best means of discovering the inner life of the play, and that the process of rehearsal, albeit based on the script, necessarily includes some aspects of improvisation.

All the following scenes for improvisation are in the nature of a problem that must be solved by groups in performance. It is the nature of this challenge – where the outline of an open-ended plot has to be thrashed out in speedy discussion, cast and performed to the other groups – that sets the adrenalin flowing and liberates students from normal inhibitions, enabling them to solve some of the technical problems of performance under studio conditions.

The discussion time allowed might vary from five to fifteen minutes, according to the nature of the scene to be presented, while the playing times might vary from five to ten minutes.

ENCOUNTERS

As a preliminary step to the group improvisations in the following section, it is useful to work on what I call encounters in which type characters meet and their temperaments or jobs lead to a dramatic situation.

The routine is as follows. The tutor has a list of type characters and allocates one to each student by simply pointing out the name from the list, without speaking. Thus no one knows what the others will characterize. Ask them to divide into groups of preferably three, but not more than four, and to take their chairs and sit well away from other groups.

When everybody is in a group, they reveal their given characters to the other members of the group. They plan a short scene, inventing situation, development, dialogue and a conclusion. At no time during the playing of any scene may any character name the temperament or occupation of themselves or anyone else. The temperaments or occupations must be revealed to the audience by means of the actions and attitudes of the performers.

At the conclusion of each short scene the players stay in the acting area while the audience discuss the behaviour of the characters and attempt to say exactly what each performer represented. The cast must not say what they were; they should have shown this.

Here are some suggestions:

Gipsy	Tax investigator
Detective	Indolent person
Traffic warden	Agitator
Deaf person	Confidence trickster
Non-stop talker	Over-modest person
Neurotic person	Scandalmonger
Boaster	Very ambitous person
Short-sighted person	Inventor
Keep-fit fanatic	Mind reader
Very shy person	Impatient person
Hypochondriac	Kleptomaniac
Do-gooder	Suspicious person
Bossy person	Flatterer
Copy-cat	Ruthless person

Very naive person
Glutton
Vain person
Imposter
Obsequious person
Fanatical gardener
Argumentative person
House-proud person
Liar
Romantic person
Quarrelsome person
Snob

Ex-convict
Supernatural being
Doctor
Very famous person
Social climber
Hard-up person
Nosy Parker
Timid person
'Holy Joe'
Foreigner
Flamboyant person
Spy

SWINDLED

This is a strong conflict situation for a group of three to five people. The group are given the basic information that one or two of them have reason to feel that they have been swindled in some way by the other members of the group.

The group have to decide:

What the alleged nature of the swindle is
Who each person is
Where they are
What happens
How it is resolved

The groups have approximately ten to fifteen minutes to agree on a situation, cast it, plan the action and arrange a rudimentary setting.

CAN I BORROW . . .?

This scene demands strong characterization and can be
played by two, three or four people.

The information given to the group is that one or two of the
group urgently wish to borrow something that is treasured by the
owners. Thus the situation is a conflict of wills.

In discussion the groups must decide:

Who these people are
What the treasured item is
Where they are
Whether intense persuasion overcomes extreme reluctance
or not

ALLERGY OR PHOBIA

This can be either a very amusing or highly dramatic scene. It
must start off in a very peaceful manner to establish the base line
of normality; something is then introduced into this tranquil
atmosphere which triggers the allergy or phobia. It can be
performed by groups of two to five people. A complication that
can be added is that one person's allergy or phobia is someone
else's delight.

The group have to decide:

Who has the allergy or phobia
What the nature of it is
Where everyone is
How the situation is resolved

Characterization and character relationships are very important
in this scene.

MORAL DILEMMA

This situation is open to a great many interpretations. Groups may be in a domestic, working or recreational setting. The given situation is that one character has to be sacrificed in some way or other for the good of the rest of the group. The scene may range in convention from comedy to tragedy.

In discussion it must be decided:

What the setting is
What everyone is doing
Why one person must be sacrificed
Who the individual characters are
How it ends

YOU'RE FIRED!

This situation generally works out as high comedy, but it could just as easily be strongly dramatic. The framework of the scene is that an applicant for a job is interviewed, given the job, shown how to do it, left to do it, makes a disastrous mistake and is fired – all in the space of five to ten minutes.

The groups must plan:

Where the job is – office, factory, hospital, etc.
What the job is
What goes wrong
The function of each character in the group

As there are at least four brief scenes, planning must be businesslike. Each scene can be represented very simply by a quick rearrangement of the basic items of furniture. The final scene, getting the sack, must be savoured as a climax.

VITAL ITEM

The setting can be domestic, recreational or work. The location can be anywhere. The group is engaged on a task when it is discovered that a vital item is missing and the task comes to a halt, as they cannot proceed without it. The missing item is found after a search. How and where it is found leads to an embarrassing, angry, amusing or frightening conclusion.

Preparation time should be generous although the scene itself may be a short one.

The groups must plan:

> The location
> The group task
> What the 'vital item' is
> Where it is found
> Which of the alternative endings to use
> The function of each character

GET RID OF IT!

Some members of the group possess something that they are desperate to get rid of. They may be trying to sell it or even to give it away.

The core of the scene is the battle of wills between those who are trying to get rid of the item and the resistance of those of the group who don't want it at any price. However, a final bit of information either makes the owners very thankful they didn't get rid of it, or else makes it irresistible to the people who, at first, refused it. This scene usually works out in terms of comedy. Concentrate on teamwork, ingenuity and characterization.

UNWELCOME VISITORS

This is a conflict situation, but one that must be handled with some delicacy; therefore there must not be any open animosity between characters, although we must sense that the visitors are most unwelcome.

The scene works well with four characters. A and B are in a certain place and are engaged in some activity which is proceeding harmoniously, when the sudden arrival of C and D shatters the atmosphere, as they are the very people A and B wish to avoid. C and D must be got rid of, but by subtle means. The characterization of the two pairs should provide a reason why A and B determine to get rid of C and D as soon as possible.

In preparation the groups must decide:

The setting
The activity of A and B
The conflict of character and interest between parties
How C and D are got rid of without open conflict

IN THE DARK

This scene can be performed with three, four or five people. The given situation is that the group is meeting to carry out an urgent job. The setting is an interior at night. Just as the group is starting to work, all the lights go out and, as they have no lighting of their own, they have to attempt to work in the dark.

Thus, the scene starts with normal visibility and then switches to pitch darkness. The object of the exercise is for the cast to appear to use only their senses of hearing and touch. This scene demands very good teamwork and the ability to remember that the eyes must not focus on anything. The movement too will become slower and more uncertain.

The interpretation can range from comedy to tragedy and, if desired, the lighting can be restored towards the end of the scene.

In the planning, particular care will have to be taken to ensure that the group pick a very clear cue so that everyone is aware that they are all suddenly in darkness.

UNAUTHORIZED ENTRY

The creation and change of mood and character relationships are the main objectives in this scene. The situation is that two or three members of the group enter a certain place without authority. While there, they are discovered by someone. At first there is a strong conflict situation, until something is done or said that completely changes the mood. The scene concludes in this new mood.

In preparation the group must plan:

The nature of the place entered without authority
The reason
Their characters and relationships
Who discovers them in this place; his or her character and attitude
What causes the mood to change
The ending

SURVIVAL

Groups of five or six are divided into two sub-groups, A and B. A are travellers lost in a very strange and remote part of the world. They encounter B, who inhabit this area and have completely different modes of communication, conduct and values. In order to survive A have to accommodate themselves to the ways of B. The scene ends when harmony is reached between the two sub-groups.

This can work as comedy or strong drama. It demands careful planning. Sub-group A speak English; sub-group B communicate in any manner they choose to devise. Concentration should be on creation of atmosphere, characterization and modes of communication.

OBSTACLE

This scene can be played by groups of four, five or even six people. The basic situation is that the group is engaged in an activity. The nature of the activity colours the mood of the scene, until the group unexpectedly encounter an obstacle of some sort, which changes the mood. When the obstacle is overcome, the mood changes once more.

The scene can be performed in any convention – comedy, farce, melodrama, tragedy. The exercise demands teamwork, ingenuity and careful planning.

In discussion the groups must plan:

The nature of the activity
The dramatic moods to be created
The obstacle encountered
How the obstacle is overcome

Preparation time for this scene should be generous.

UNPLEASANT ENCOUNTER

This exercise for pairs gives opportunities for development of character and character relationships.

The given situation is that two people, who detest one another, find themselves stuck in each other's company. It is the very different characters of these two people which has given rise to this animosity.

During the time these two are in one another's presence they can either develop the most tremendous row or else find that, although they are very different types with different views, they must bury the hatchet, because during the initial row a misunderstanding has been revealed.

The scene needs very careful planning and differentiation of characters.

COURT SCENE

Court scenes usually have an element of drama built into them arising from the conflicting interests of the prosecution and defence. The scene may be planned either in a Magistrates' Court or a Crown Court, which will require a larger cast for the jury and extra legal personnel. The tutor needs to gain some idea of legal procedures, but, as the purpose of the work is to develop acting techniques, some licence may be permitted. Visits to Magistrates' and Crown Courts are most helpful.

If the total group is large enough it may be divided into two, with one half acting as jury for the prepared case of the other half and then, after completion of the first case, changing roles.

Preparation time must be generous and the following points must be decided:

The offence being tried
The appropriate court for that sort of offence

The cast, including accused, witnesses and legal personnel
The sequence of procedures
The physical layout of the court

DID YOU HEAR THAT?

In this scene the emphasis is on auditory sensation and the very different reactions from individual characters. The setting may be domestic, occupational or recreational. The circumstances are that each member of the group says he, or she, can hear a certain sort of noise. Everyone hears something different. The noise also provokes a different reaction from each. At a predetermined point in the action the group are forced to investigate. When they discover the cause each visualizes something quite different.

Timing will need to be subtle with good use of pauses. As the convention of this scene approximates to fantasy the conclusion should be appropriate.

STREET SCENE

This scene requires a group of at least eight to twelve people to make it work properly. The setting is a broad pavement in front of a large store or a station. One person accidently drops a valuable item. Other people in the area try to pick it up without anyone else seeing them, but are always frustrated by passers-by. Finally one character manages to get hold of it and is just about to pocket it when he or she is spotted by the loser who has been searching for it. The would-be thief is thanked and the owner goes off with the item.

This exercise calls for very careful timing and co-ordination. Each person must know exactly when to come into the action and when to drift out of it. Many of the characters may be in the acting area for a lot of the time, but must make their presence unobtrusive when they are not responsible for the current action.

BITER BIT

The possibilities for interpreting this theme are very wide indeed. Although groups often perform it in terms of comedy, it works well as strong drama, melodrama or even fantasy. The circumstances are that three or four characters decide to steal a certain item or just 'borrow' it without the knowledge of the owner. When the item is in their possession, they open the container in which they believed the item was kept. The contents of the container have a most alarming or unusual effect.
In planning the group will have to decide:

What they imagine the item is
Why they want it
Who the characters are
The setting
What the item turns out to be
What it does to them
The conclusion

READING THE WILL

In the scene to be improvised, the exercise is to devise a will reading where the known expectations of the characters are reversed, but where their feelings are expressed in a very subtle manner – so that although we know that someone must be bitterly resentful, or very pleased, feelings are under control and on the surface all proceeds with decorum.

The aim of the exercise is to help to develop depth of characterization and to teach the student to convey strong emotions by subtle means. Before the reading of the will characters may show their expectations freely, but afterwards the audience must sense what they feel by their intonation and by subtle physical reactions rather than by what they demonstrate on the surface.

CAUGHT IN THE ACT

For this scene groups of three, four or five divide themselves into either 'culprits' or 'catchers'. In the discussion time the groups have to decide the act in which the 'culprits' are discovered by the 'catchers', the setting in which it takes place and the function of each character. The twist is that the 'culprits' turn out to be the innocent party.

Discussion time for this scene may need to be more generous than the usual ten minutes.

THIS CAN'T BE THE PLACE

This exercise is in two parts. In the first scene, the group of, say, three to five characters are either planning a visit somewhere or are actually travelling there. During this scene they reveal their expectations of their destination. The second scene shows the arrival of the group at this destination. It turns out to be very different from what was anticipated in the first scene. The group must show how the characters adjust to these unexpected circumstances and also how each person's character is revealed by his or her reactions.

WRONG DELIVERY

This scene works with groups of three to five people. It can take place in a working or domestic setting. The first few minutes of the scene must establish exactly where the group is and what each character's function is. When these facts have been established, a letter, telegram or message is wrongly delivered which is opened by mistake. From then on there is pandemonium; the previously established atmosphere is shattered. After a few minutes the mistake is realized, but the former relatively peaceful mood cannot be restored, because things have been said and done that will make this impossible.

The mood changes need careful planning and timing and the reason for the change in relationships must be made very clear.

STOLEN PROPERTY FOR SALE

This can also be in a domestic or working situation and works with three to five people.

The situation is that some item has been advertised for sale. A phone call establishes that somebody wants to see it. Preparations are made to display the item to the best advantage. The prospective buyer arrives to inspect the object for sale and declares that it is identical to an item recently stolen. From this moment on the atmosphere changes from one of cordiality to one of conflict.

In discussion the groups must decide:

    The characters of all concerned
    The setting
    The item for sale
    How the conflict is resolved

EXHIBITION

In this scene the concentration should be on developing naturalistic characters and avoiding the temptation to approximate to 'types'.

This exercise requires groups of six to eight people. The setting is an exhibition – of painting, sculpture, fashion or furniture, for example. The planning discussion will have to include the characters of the people attending the exhibition and the way in which they reveal their attitudes towards the exhibits and each other. Also, attention should be paid to the dovetailing of dialogue and the co-ordination of movement. These are things that develop as a group continues to work together, so sensitivity to the flow of action and dialogue should be encouraged. The phasing of the entry of performers into the exhibition area must be thought about, as well as the final grouping in the exhibition area, where on a verbal cue all will freeze in the manner of a tableau that should further help to reveal the nature of the characters, which the audience will discuss.

TERMINUS

This exercise needs groups of at least ten people. It is a 'slice of life', lasting about five minutes. As in EXHIBITION it is an exercise in naturalism.

The scene is a main-line railway station or an air terminal. Each person is a naturalistic character – either working or travelling – with possibly one or two eccentric characters. The flow of movement and grouping must be planned so that the audience can see right into the situation without masking. Also dialogue should dovetail and not overlap, unless it is intended to do so. At a predetermined cue all characters freeze for an evaluation of the performance.

GOSSIP

Groups of five work best for this exercise, which encourages the use of fantasy. It is best not to have any preliminary discussion period at all, as the performers, who will enter the acting area in sequence, will have to decide what they are going to contribute to the scene by listening to the dialogue of the pair on stage; they will then enter and elaborate on what they have heard when one of the performers leaves. This is the way it works. Character A encounters B in a public area, where people can meet freely. A tells B something extraordinary about E, the final member of the group to enter, and then has to leave. C then enters, is greeted by B, and in the course of conversation tells C, with great elaboration, what A has just said about E. B then has to go. When C is alone D comes on and C elaborates on what B has said about E, so that the original bit of information is quite distorted. C then leaves and D is alone in the acting area when E enters and greets D. The end of the scene is the encounter between D and E. They have to decide at the moment of meeting what one will say to the other and what their mutual reactions are to be. It is up to E, of course, to bring the scene to some sort of conclusion.

TRAIN OF EVENTS

This scene offers an opportunity to develop quick responses and to show inventiveness. Almost any number of actors from two to twelve can work in this situation.

The given conditions are simply that an apparently insignificant action, or statement, at the beginning of the scene triggers off a train of events that, like a snowball rolling downhill, leads the scene to a momentous conclusion. Thus the scene starts very quietly and then builds up to an explosive ending.

The setting can be almost anywhere in place or time and the style can be in any dramatic convention.

IT'S LOCKED

Within most dramatic situations there is, necessarily, some sort of tension or conflict, even if it is very subtle. In this scene the conflict is between the members of the cast as well as between them and an object. The set-up is that a door – it could be the door to a room, cupboard, safe, loft, cellar or anything else – apparently can't be opened. The conflict is therefore between the shut door and those who wish to open it and those who wish it to remain shut.

The groups of two to six people must decide in discussion:

What and where this door is
Who these characters are
Why some wish to open it and some do not
Whether the door has ever been opened
If it has, what is on the other side
How whatever is on the other side affects people
How the situation is resolved

TYRANT

This scene works with groups from two to eight. The given circumstances are that within the group there is one strong character who dominates and to whom all the others are entirely subservient. During the action the subservient characters discover something about the dominant person that could release them from this intolerable situation.

During the planning session the group must decide:

The setting
The function of the individual characters
Why it was possible for one person to dominate

What is found out about the dominant character
Whether they use this knowledge to overthrow the tyrant

The characters should be naturalistic and guard against the situation becoming melodramatic.

OBSESSION

The group, from three to ten people, are travelling in some means of enclosed public transport, so that they cannot get off until the destination is reached. This might be a plane, a railway carriage, a cable car or a boat, for example.

One of the characters has an obsession that only becomes evident after the travellers are well on their way. This obsession affects each character in a different way. Some may be amused, others horrified, disgusted, puzzled or indifferent.

In this scene there is scope to explore almost any convention – naturalism, fantasy, melodrama or even tragedy.

At the conclusion of the exercise it should be possible for the audience to differentiate the reactions of characters and comment on the convention.

TRAVELLERS ANONYMOUS

This scene, like the last one, is set in some means of enclosed public transport. Groups may vary in size from five to eight people. The travellers take their seats for the journey. They do not speak or acknowledge one another's presence. They mind their own business and are preoccupied with their own particular activities.

When they are on their way some incident rouses the characters from their personal preoccupations and they start talking and interacting with sufficient lack of reserve to show the audience their characters in full.

At the end of the scene the cast freeze into a tableau for a short time while the audience discuss the characters that have been revealed.

ROOM TO LET

The setting for this scene is domestic. A family of two or three people have a room to let and in the first few minutes of the scene the general background of the family and the reason for letting the room are revealed. In response to an advertisement someone is coming to see the room – so the setting should represent the living-room of the family and the room to be let. With the arrival of the applicant there are introductions all round, some questions and answers and then the applicant is shown the room and left to browse around it. Meanwhile someone has recognized the applicant and tells the rest of the family all about this person. This information leads to a heated discussion at the end of which the applicant returns to the living-room.

In preparation the group must decide:

On the characters in the family
The character of the applicant for the room
The nature of the information revealed
The reactions of the family to that information
Whether the room is let to that person or not
If not, how the applicant is dealt with

THE ADMIRABLE CRICHTON

The theme of Barrie's play is that a humble member of a group, who is not considered to be of much importance, is found to possess qualities and knowledge that save them all in an emergency.

Groups can vary from five to ten people. In discussion each group will have to decide:

Where they are
What they are doing in that place
Who each character is
The nature of the emergency that arises
Why only the character the rest consider to be of no importance is capable of dealing with the emergency
Whether the status structure of the group alters after the emergency or stays the same

The scene should be played naturalistically and with great attention to characterization.

AN ANCIENT CUSTOM

This scene, which deals with creation and changes of mood, needs firm characterization and careful timing. Groups may vary from two to six characters. Each group is divided into two sections, A and B. The two sections come from very different backgrounds, with completely different customs. They are meeting for a social or business occasion, but as their knowledge of each other's language is sketchy there are some misunderstandings.

At some point during the meeting, when things seem to be going particularly well, one of the parties says or does something that completely outrages the other half of the group. This leads to a tremendous row. However, tempers die down and tranquillity is restored when the offending party manages to explain that no offence was intended, that it is an ancient custom of their country and indeed a great compliment. Thus, the scene begins in a peaceful mood, goes through a period of tension, which is eased, and ends as calmly as it began.

ANGRY COMPLAINT

This is an excellent exercise for letting go and externalizing emotions. The core of the scene is the battle of wills between the two combatants. It is a test of concentration, quick thinking and determination.

The setting is any kind of shop or place where a service is rendered. Character A is the customer or client and character B is the person responsible for running the establishment. A counter, desk or bench can be represented by a table dividing the acting area. On one side is the person who runs the establishment, in position before the furious customer enters from the other side. The customer, A, confronts B with a complaint about something purchased or a service rendered. B refutes the charge and the argument rages.

At first neither side may give in but, as the scene must have a time limit, a decision has to be reached – such as the manager reluctantly agreeing to a refund, or the customer having to admit that the item was wrongly used and having to back down. It may end in threats of legal proceedings. When the time limit has been reached the tutor should call a halt.

In the discussion period A and B must decide:

What sort of establishment it is
Who is to be A and who B
What is being complained about

How the scene ends (alternatively, the ending may be unplanned and A and B will try to batter each other into submission by verbal duelling)

As may be imagined this scene stimulates quick-fire repartee and more often than not emerges as comedy.

CAN YOU HELP ME . . .?

This scene is also a battle of wills between two combatants, A and B. They meet in the centre of the acting area where a very determined A will require the assistance of the reluctant B.

A is the only character who is prepared – knowing what to ask and what tactics to use. B is quite unprepared, only knowing that he or she must avoid complying with the request if at all possible. The B characters are picked at random by the tutor to act as 'victims' for the A characters.

The scene demands quick thinking and reactions, the marshalling of ideas, and force in putting them across. It is important not to let the scene continue until it flags, but to let it reach a reasonable conclusion, even if it is simply B shouting, 'No!' to A and making a strong exit.

FOREIGN SHOPPING

This scene operates with groups of three people. It is almost invariably a demanding and amusing exercise, both for the performers and the spectators.

The situation is that character A is a foreigner who speaks no recognizable language but utters series of sounds of his or her own invention – in fact, gibberish. Shopkeepers B and C speak English to each other and to the customer, A, who, of course, must appear not to understand a word.

The setting is a table set in the middle of the acting area. This represents the counter of a shop and is so positioned that all gestures and movements made by the three characters are clearly visible to the audience. There must be no masking.

The shop is a supershop which sells absolutely everything – nothing is too big or too small. B and C are in position behind their counter before A enters. A comes into the shop and tries to make himself or herself understood, but is incomprehensible to B and C, who may say so. A cannot leave the shop without the article B and C sell – for there is nothing they do not sell – so he or she has to resort to mime and to making onomatopoeic sounds to try and show what he or she wants. B and C must talk to each other clearly enough for the audience to hear if they do not understand what is wanted, or if they think that A might want a certain article. Also, A must be able to hear what B and C are going to offer as a result of his or her mime. As an example, after a few moments of miming, B might say to C, 'I think she wants a bicycle! Get a bicycle!' C goes to the back of the shop and mimes wheeling a bicycle out to A, saying to B, 'Well, there's a bicycle for her.' If A doesn't want a bicycle, she shoos it away and C removes it. If A does want a bicycle, but only a racing bicycle will do, she may make semi-approving noises and mime using a racing bicycle with low-swept handlebars. B may say to C, 'Get her a racing bicycle.' When C brings out the racing bicycle, A appears only half pleased as it's the wrong colour – she wants a red one. So she points to somebody's red socks. When C brings the red racing bike A is delighted and wheels it off. End of scene.

Only the A characters know what they are going to buy from the supershop. Shopkeepers B and C are deliberately picked at random from the group. The interesting thing about this exercise is that very often the audience know what A wants before B and C do. Further, when A fails to communicate, he or she has to keep on refining and repeating his or her request until it is so clear that B and C cannot fail to understand.

HIGH-PRESSURE SALES

This scene for groups of four or five people is an exercise in characterization and teamwork.

The given situation is that a high-pressure salesperson has bulldozed his or her way into the home of a quiet and unresisting family to demonstrate and sell his or her product to these people, who seem to be quite overwhelmed by the slick sales technique. At the conclusion of the sales routine the salesperson feels that he or she has it all sewn up and has only to get the signature on the order form, or the cash. However, at the very moment of anticipated success something occurs which causes the salesperson to leave in a hurry.

The salesperson must be a true character and not a caricature, and the members of the family, although quiet people, must each be quite individual. Moreover, the occurrence that makes the salesperson leave must be plausible.

REVELATION

This scene, also for groups of four or five people, can be set in a domestic or working situation.

The group is engaged in its normal domestic or working routine, which must be established in the first few minutes. The audience must have time to form an impression of the individual characters and their relationships, and to savour the harmonious atmosphere. The harmony of the group is disturbed, however, when one, or possibly two, of its members are unexpectedly revealed to be different from what the others imagined them to be. This revelation leads to a crisis in the relationships within the group.

Things to be decided in the planning time are:

The situation within which the group operates

The setting
The characters and their relationships
The nature of the revelation
The crisis
How the crisis is resolved

WE DON'T LIKE TO ASK, BUT . . .

This is a character-conflict situation for four actors. The group is divided into two sections – A and B. The two characters in section A detest the two characters in section B. Section B returns this feeling wholeheartedly. At the beginning of the scene the reasons why A and B dislike one another so much must be made clear. The situation is complicated by A being compelled to request a very great favour from B. The core of the scene is how A are going to approach B, overcome the mutual antagonisms and have the favour granted.

In discussion the characters must decide:

The background to the situation
The favour requested and the means used to get it
The nature of the four characters
The conclusion

OFFICIAL ENCOUNTER

Although this scene may be interpreted in a variety of ways, from conflict to concord between the official and the non-official characters, the majority of groups seem to get more dramatic mileage out of conflict situations.

The given circumstances are simply that the officials and the non-officials meet in a certain place, under certain circumstances, and this encounter generates a dramatic situation. This bare framework must be fleshed out by the individual groups to create a satisfying drama.

The groups must decide:

Who these officials and non-officials are
The setting in which the scene takes place
How the encounter takes place
The result of the encounter

7

Imagination and Dramatic Truth

This section is less structured and places greater demands on imagination and unobtrusive use of technique. The essential quality of dramatic truth must be established in whatever convention a scene is performed.

IT'S ANYTHING BUT . . .

The assembled group, sitting in a semi-circle as an audience, have placed in the acting area before them a recognizable everyday article. It might be a telephone, a bucket, small table, armchair or any property that can provide sufficient challenge for this particular exercise.

The tutor says something like, 'At the moment you may think that that thing there is an old vacuum cleaner, but it is not. It is anything you care to imagine, but it is not a vacuum cleaner. With your imagination, sense of fantasy and dramatic truth I want you to look at this thing and visualize it as something quite different. It can be animate or inanimate, larger or smaller, heavier or lighter, made from any material and quite a different shape. You have up to five minutes to transform this thing with the aid of your imagination into some other thing with which you are going to act, using dialogue if you wish, for a few moments. Your task is to make us feel that you are really visualizing this as the transformed object.'

This is a popular exercise giving actors the chance to display visual imagery, concentration and virtuosity.

SOME THING

This exercise for pairs is related to IT'S ANYTHING BUT. . .; however, instead of a commonplace property, actor A uses another actor, B, as anything except a person. The 'thing', B, is unprepared, but briefed that he or she must be completely flexible so that he or she can be moulded into any possible shape and moved if necessary. Thus A may decide to make B into an anti-aircraft gun, a petrol pump, telephone, fruit machine, etc.

The A characters can be allowed three to four minutes to plan their routine. The B 'things' are picked at random by the tutor from anywhere in the group so what we see demonstrated will only be the work of A characters. Dialogue can be used if appropriate.

FIRST AND LAST

This exercise requires very flexible use of the imagination in utilizing verbal clues to create a dramatic scene.

The tutor asks the members of the assembled group to think of any short sentence or phrase. When, after a minute or so, everybody has had time to think of one, the tutor asks each person in turn to say their sentence or phrase. When the tutor has heard them all, he or she picks one that sounds as if it could stimulate the imagination and then memorizes it. He or she then asks people to think of a second short sentence or phrase and memorizes one of them. Groups of about four performers are then asked to plan a short scene, playing for not more than five minutes, in which one of the selected sentences or phrases is used at the beginning of the scene and the other at the end.

There is no restriction on the possibilities of interpretation.

FOUR WORDS

In a similar way to the previous exercise, the tutor invites each member of the group to volunteer a sentence of four words. The sentences offered must be strongly dynamic and invite dramatic interpretation.

The aim is to create a powerful scene of not more than five minutes' duration.

THIS AND THIS AND THIS

In this scene the stimuli are objects instead of words. The tutor places a number of properties in the acting area – from three to six should do – and invites all the members of the group to examine them, as they are to be used in a short scene, of any convention, either as the things they really are or as some other object. Allow generous time for preparation.

PLACE, MOOD, OBJECT

For this exercise the tutor asks all the members of the group to name a place where dramatic action can take place. From those offered he or she selects one and remembers it. The tutor then asks the group to suggest the dominant mood and, lastly, an

object. From the place, mood and object, selected by the tutor
for their dramatic possibilities, smaller groups devise and act a
scene in any convention, lasting not more than five minutes.

WHAT HAPPENED?

This is another problem to be solved by dramatic means. In the
acting area is a collection of furniture and properties. They are
not set to represent a room in good order but are in a state of
disarray. Some items, for example, might be on their side,
upside down or piled up one on top of the other. The task of the
whole group is to examine, as individuals, this disarray silently
for some minutes and then to divide into small groups of four to
six people. These small groups re-examine the setting, discuss
it, memorize where items are placed and then plan a short scene
in which the furniture and properties end up in the manner set
by the tutor.

The task therefore is to plan:

How they are set initially and what they represent
The short dramatic situation in that setting
The individual characters and their functions
The climax that leaves the set in disarray

A variation on this exercise, which may be performed without
a setting if desired, is to give the final visual image of the scene,
such as the members of the group in a tableau, fighting, feeling
ill or frightened, celebrating or rushing off quickly.

SENSATIONS

Although the use of the five senses is demonstrated in the normal practice of improvisation, this exercise gives scope for concentration on the dramatic use of the senses: sight, smell, sound, taste and touch. It emphasizes the importance of allowing the audience to savour the sensory stimulation generated by the performer.

Small groups of two or three will give the audience more choice of observing and offering constructive comment afterwards.

About four examples of the operation of a particular sense can be shown in each scene:

Smell: Cooking, gas, smoke, perfume
Sight: Attraction, repulsion, amazement, distant object
Sound: Cry, shot, music, doorbell
Taste: Sickly medicine, fine wine, hot curry, doubtful food
Touch: Rough, sticky, silky, light or heavy

Timing should be careful to allow the sensations generated to be transmitted to and appreciated by the audience. Of course, the result of the sensations will not be confined to the organ concerned, but will be reflected by involuntary physical reactions.

INSTANT ACTING

This is an exercise that can be used at almost any stage of a drama course – as a game to break down inhibitions; as an exercise to encourage students to leap into a dramatic situation that requires them to think and react with great speed; or as an exercise to maintain the idea of spontaneity and to explore dramatic possibilities and character interaction. It is always great fun and makes the adrenalin flow.

The whole group, of say twelve to twenty people, sit in a circle sufficiently large to enclose an acting area of at least fourteen feet in diameter.

The tutor moves around the inside of the circle indicating the pairs who will work together in the centre of the circle – AB, AB, AB, etc. If the group makes an odd number, a threesome can be formed at the end. The tutor then asks everybody to think of an order that they can call out to the pair in the centre. It must be a simple everyday activity that they would be prepared to do themselves. It should be phrased clearly and spoken loudly, so that the people in the centre know exactly what they have to do and can jump into the situation without a moment's hesitation. Pairs will enter the acting area in turn, have an order called out to them and immediately plunge into the action. If the scene requires chairs, the pair can grab their own chairs, but everything else is mimed. As there is no preparation the scenes will be limited to a few minutes. Each pair will have two orders to enact. The tutor says 'First order,' 'Second order,' and, finally, 'Thank you, next pair please.' The routine works swiftly with no long pauses between pairs. When a pair receives an order, one performer is usually seen to seize the initiative a fraction of a second before the other, thus deciding his or her own role, with the partner obligingly supplying the complementary character.

When students are used to this game, orders can become more sophisticated. Occasionally what has been started by a pair becomes so well developed and compelling to watch that one is inclined to allow it to run on in order to see what happens.

SUBTEXT

The aim of this exercise is to encourage performers to use voice and speech with subtlety, depth of meaning, careful timing and variety. It is intended to combat what I call 'speaking print', where casts faithfully render the printed dialogue, but without communicating in depth by allowing the voice to explore the full spectrum of meaning within, or under, the text.

The group is divided into pairs and each pair plans a short scene about a normal everyday type of activity – such as buying clothes or learning to drive a car. It should be something in which there is, necessarily, a certain amount of movement. The pair must prepare the sequence of events carefully, so that each knows what the other is supposed to be talking about or doing. The idea is that, instead of normal language, they are to use a sequence of numbers, days of the week or months of the year, to convey by intonation, timing and gesture what they *feel* about the thing they are discussing or doing. Thus the sounds used by performer A, with appropriate intonation, timing and gesture, might be '1-234-5-6-7-8?' implying the possible meaning, 'What do you think of my new hat?' B might reply, '1-2-3-45?', meaning to A, 'Where did you get it?', but at the same time, by means of intonation, timing, gesture and facial expression, conveying to the audience that in B's private opinion it is a monstrosity.

At the end of each scene the audience and the performers confer on the communication conveyed by the intonation, timing, gestures and facial expressions.

Short arguments and love scenes work well in this context.

INTERPRETATIONS

This exercise for pairs is related to SUBTEXT, as it encourages the performer to savour the full implication behind the words uttered. The dialogue of these very short scenes is deliberately ambiguous. The scene has to be given a meaning and that meaning is conveyed by the tone, volume, pace and variety of the voice, together with the timing of the actions and the reactions of the characters. There is no need for any setting or props – these must be created by the imagination.

As the written dialogue is so brief, the substance of the interpretation must be clarified by movement, gesture, timing, stillness and silence. There may be a great deal of action, with the dialogue interspersed like currants in a bun, or the action may preceed, follow or alternate with dialogue.

There is sometimes a tendency in student performances to press on with the dialogue, to get through speeches, 'speaking print'. This exercise helps to concentrate the mind on total communication.

1. A: You
   B: Yes
   A: What are you doing here?
   B: I came to see you

2. A: Who is that?
   B: It's me. Open the door
   A: Did you get it?
   B: Yes
   A: Let's see it

3. A: Excuse me. Aren't you Mr/Mrs . . .?
   B: Mr/Mrs . . .?
   A: Yes

4. A: Come over here
   B: But it is . . .
   A: Of course

5. A: Take that
   B: What?
   A: Will you please . . .

6. A: Is it there?
   B: Yes
   A: Quick
   B: Hold on

7. A: I knew
   B: Did you?
   A: Yes
   B: Oh

8: A: Look
   B: Incredible
   A: Pleased?
   B: Mmm

9. A: Not easy
   B: Now
   A: Careful
   B: Don't

10. A: This is the last
    B: You're sure?
    A: Definitely
    B: What's that?

11. A: Can you see?
    B: Good heavens
    A: What is . . .
    B: That's better

12. A: I'm sorry
    B: Turn round

A: All right?

B: Trust you

13. A: No

B: I thought you might

A: Oh

B: Splendid

14. A: It just makes me angry

B: It's really very simple

A: Shall I try again?

B: There you are

15. A: Why do you . . .

B: Did I do that?

A: Try again

B: Oh

16. A: It won't work

B: Come and look at this

A: My God . . .

B: What do we do now?

17. A: Is there much?

B: Enough

A: Fantastic

B: Look out

18. A: Right . . .

B: Are you quite sure?

A: What did I tell you?

B: I can't move it

19. A: I don't believe it
    B: It's been a long time
    A: Do you remember that?
    B: Yes. I also remember something else

20. A: I'm not sure of the way it goes
    B: Try the other way
    A: This is very nice
    B: Use some of this

21. A: I found this
    B: What can it be?
    A: Hold that and I'll unscrew . . .
    B: That was a narrow escape

22. A: What do you think you're doing?
    B: Oh – sorry
    A: It's not as easy as you think
    B: Help me with it

23. A: It makes you look – peculiar
    B: What about that then?
    A: Oh – that's better. Fix this for me
    B: Where are they? Help me. Oh

24. A: Now
    B: How about?
    A: Think I'm going to be . . .
    B: Sorry

8

Scenes for Rehearsal

Aristophanes

Lysistrata
(Penguin, London)
Act 1
Lysistrata, Calonice, Myrrhine
and Lampito
Lysistrata: 'Just think if it had
been a Bacchic celebration' . . .
Calonice: 'We must show that it's
not for nothing that women are
called impossible.'

Ayckbourn, Alan

Round and Round the Garden
(Penguin, London)
Act 1, Scene 1
Annie and Norman
Annie: 'Hallo? Anyone about?'
. . . 'I'll have a bath before I leave.'

*

Act 2, Scene 1
Ruth, Sarah and Tom
Ruth: 'Well.' . . . 'Hasn't got her
glasses on.'

Beckett, Samuel

Waiting for Godot
(Faber and Faber, London)
Act 2
Estragon and Vladimir

98

Estragon: 'In the meantime let us try and converse calmly'. . . 'That wasn't such a bad little canter.'

Bowen, John

Little Boxes: Trevor
(Methuen, London)
Sarah, Trevor and Jane
Sarah: 'Shall I take your coat?'. . .
Jane: 'No. I did.'

Brecht, Bertolt

The Caucasian Chalk Circle
(Penguin, London)
Scene 1
Simon and Grusha
Simon: 'Grusha! There you are at last!' . . . 'I thank you, Grusha Vashnadze. And good-bye!'

*

Scene 3
Grusha, Ironshirt and Simon
Grusha: 'Simon!' . . . 'Leave him here. Please! He's mine!'

Camus, Albert

Caligula
(Penguin, London)
Act 4
Caesonia and Caligula
Caesonia: 'What are you thinking about?' to end of play.

Capek, Karel and Joseph

The Life of the Insects
(Dent, London)
Act 2
Crysalis, Vagrant, Male Beetle, Female Beetle, Ichneumon Fly, Larva, Male Cricket, Female

Cricket, Parasite and Strange Beetle
The whole scene or various duologues.

Chekhov, Anton

The Bear
(Penguin, London)
Popov and Smirnov
Smirnov: 'Pay me back my money' . . . Popov: 'I hate you. I . . . challenge you!' (A prolonged kiss). Omit Looka references.

Uncle Vania
(Penguin, London)
Act 3
Sonia and Yeliena
Sonia: 'Autumn roses, exquisite, mournful' . . . 'Nothing.' (Goes out).

The Cherry Orchard
(Penguin, London)
Act 4
Varia and Lopahin
Varia: (Starts examining luggage) 'It's strange, I just can't find' . . . (Varia alone, sobs softly).

Cooper, Giles

Everything in the Garden
(Penguin, London)
Act 1
Jenny and Bernard
From beginning of act . . . Bernard: 'Yes, do come in, my wife's in here.'

*

Act 1
Jenny and Leonie
Jenny: 'Good evening.' . . .
Leonie: '. . . ten o'clock in the
morning please.'

Coward, Noel

Blythe Spirit
(Samuel French, London)
Act 2, Scene 2
Ruth and Madame Arcati
Madame Arcati: 'My dear Mrs
Condomine' . . . Ruth: 'Damn –
Damn – Damn!'

Delaney, Shelagh

A Taste of Honey
(Methuen, London)
Act 1, Scene 1
Helen and Jo
Helen: 'Well! This is the place.'
. . . Jo: 'You never do anything for
me.'

*

Act 1, Scene 1
Helen, Jo and Peter
Helen: 'Oh! My God! Look what
the wind's blown in.' . . . 'Come
on.'

Farquhar, George

The Beaux' Stratagem
(Pan Books, London)
Act 2, Scene 1
Dorinda and Mrs Sullen
Dorinda: 'Morrow, my dear sister'
. . . Mrs Sullen: '. . . he will beg
my pardon.'

Frisch, Max

The Fire Raisers
(Methuen, London)
Scene 1
Biedermann, Anna and Schmitz
Anna: 'Herr Biedermann?' . . .
Biedermann: 'My wife has a weak
heart –'

Genet, Jean

The Balcony
(Faber and Faber, London)
Scene 3
General and Girl
General: '. . . And you're late.
Where the hell . . .' Girl: '. . . The
military band plays a funeral
march.'

Giraudoux, Jean

The Madwoman of Chaillot
(Dramatists Play Service, Inc.,
New York)
Act 2
Countess and the Sewer Man
Sewer Man: 'Countess!' . . .
'. . . Not even rats.'

Gogol, Nikolai

The Government Inspector
(Heinemann, London)
Act 3, Scene 1
Marya, Hlestakov and Anna
Marya: (Seeing Hlestakov) 'Oh!'
. . . '. . . I won't do it again,
Mummy, really I won't.'

Grass, Günter

Flood
(Penguin, London)
Act 1

Pearl and Point, two rats.
Pearl: 'Tell me a little story, Point.'
. . . Point: '. . . The whole lot of
them – even the cats.'

Hampton, Christopher

The Philanthropist
(Faber and Faber, London)
Scene 4
Araminta, Celia and Philip
Araminta: 'Er, hello' to end of
scene.

Ibsen, Henrik

Ghosts
(Penguin, London)
Act 1
Regina and Engstrand
Regina (Lowering her voice):
'What do you want?'. . . Engstrand:
'I can prove it by the parish
register.'

Hedda Gabler
(Penguin, London)
Act 2
Hedda and Brack
Hedda: 'How do you do again, Mr
Brack?' . . . '. . . And so the train
goes on.'

Ionesco, Eugène

Amédée or How to Get Rid of It
(Penguin, London)
Act 1
Madeleine and Amédée
Madeleine: 'What do you think
you're doing?' . . . Amédée: 'He's
branching out.'

Miller, Arthur

Death of a Salesman
(Penguin, London)
Act 1
Happy and Biff
Happy: 'Funny, Biff, y'know?'
... '... have a good talk with
him.'

Molière

The Would-be Gentleman
(Penguin, London)
Act 2
Mr Jourdain and Philosopher
Philosopher: 'Let us come to our
lesson.' ... 'You may rely upon
me, sir.'

Tartuffe
(Penguin, London)
Act 3
Tartuffe and Elmire
Tartuffe: 'May the bounty of
Heaven' ... Elmire: '... con-
cerned with anything here below.'

Mortimer, John

Lunch Hour
(Samuel French, London)
Manageress, Man and Girl
Manageress: 'I've found a shilling
for you' to end of play.

Orton, Joe

Entertaining Mr Sloane
(Eyre Methuen, London)
Act 1
Kath and Sloane
Kath: 'All right, Mr Sloane? Help
yourself' to end of Act 1.

Loot
(Eyre Methuen, London)
Act 1
Fay and Truscott
Truscott: 'Good afternoon' . . . 'I think that's all I want from you, miss.'

Osborne, John

Look Back in Anger
(Faber and Faber, London)
Act 1
Jimmy, Cliff and Alison
Jimmy: 'Why do I do this every Sunday?' . . . '. . . and that we're actually alive.'

Pinter, Harold

Betrayal
(Eyre Methuen, London)
Scene 3
Jerry and Emma
The whole scene.

A Night Out
(Eyre Methuen, London)
Act 1, Scene 1
Mother and Albert
The whole scene.

Night School
(Methuen, London)
Annie, Walter and Milly
Annie: 'Look at your raincoat' . . .
Walter: 'She's taking you for a ride.'

Priestley, J. B.

An Inspector Calls
(Samuel French, London)
Act 2
Inspector, Mrs Birling, Sheila and
Birling
Mrs Birling: 'You have a photo-
graph of the girl?' . . . Sheila:
'Now, mother – don't you see?'

Sartre, Jean-Paul

In Camera
(Penguin, London)
Estelle, Inez and Garcin
Garcin: 'You're wrong. So long as
each' . . . 'Yes, perhaps a trifle
better.'

Shaffer, Peter

Black Comedy
(Samuel French, London)
Carol and Brindsley
Brindsley: 'There! How you you
think the room' . . . 'Perhaps they'll
have some candles as well.'

Shakespeare, William

Hamlet
(Penguin, London)
Act 3, Scene 1
Hamlet and Ophelia
Hamlet: 'Soft you now! The fair
Ophelia' . . . Ophelia: '. . . what
I have seen, see what I see.'

Shaw, Bernard

Arms and the Man
(Penguin, London)
Act 1
Man and Raina
Man: 'A narrow shave but a miss

is as . . .' . . . 'Not to lie down either, only sit down. Ah!'

The Doctor's Dilemma
(Penguin, London)
Act 1
Ridgeon, Redpenny and Mrs Dubedat
Ridgeon: 'Redpenny!' . . . Mrs Dubedat: '. . . I know you will cure him. Goodbye.'

Sheridan, Richard Brinsley

The Rivals
(Samuel French, London)
Act 1, Scene 2
Lydia, Mrs Malaprop and Sir Anthony Absolute
Mrs Malaprop: 'There, Sir Anthony, sits the . . .' to end of scene.

Stoppard, Tom

Enter a Free Man
(Faber and Faber, London)
Act 1
Persephone, Riley and Linda
Persephone: (Vacuum cleaning) 'Move your foot' . . . Linda: 'Ma! Are you bringing the tea!'

Wilde, Oscar

The Importance of Being Earnest
(Penguin, London)
Act 2
Cecily and Gwendolen
Cecily: 'Pray let me introduce myself' . . . Gwendolen: '. . . social spheres have been widely different.'

Williams, Tennessee   *A Streetcar Named Desire*
                               (Penguin, London)
                               Scene 10
                               Blanche and Stanley
                               The whole scene.

Wymark, Olwen   *We Three*
                               (in *Play Ten*, Edward Arnold,
                               London)
                               Em, Bridie and Girl
                               Em: 'I'm here. I'm sorry I'm late'
                               to end of play.

Bibliography

ACTING

Barker, Clive, *Theatre Games*, Eyre Methuen, London, 1977.

Barkworth, Peter, *About Acting*, Secker and Warburg, London, 1980.

Barkworth, Peter, *More about Acting*, Secker and Warburg, London, 1984.

Barton, John, *Playing Shakespeare*, Methuen, London and New York, 1984.

Cole, Toby, *Acting: A Handbook of the Stanislavski Method*, Crown Publishers Inc., New York, 1955.

Cole, Toby and Chinoy, Helen Krich, *Actors on Acting*, Crown Publishers Inc., New York, 1970.

Hayman, Ronald, *Techniques of Acting*, Eyre Methuen, London, 1969.

Stanislavski, Konstantin, *An Actor Prepares*, Geoffrey Bles, London, 1937.

—— *An Actor's Handbook*, Theatre Arts Books, New York, 1963.

—— *Building a Character*, Eyre Methuen, London, 1979.

—— *Creating a Role*, Theatre Arts Books, New York, 1961.

IMPROVISATION

Hodgson, John and Richards, Ernest, *Improvisation*, Eyre Methuen, London, 1966.

Johnstone, Keith, *Impro*, Eyre Methuen, London, 1981.

Spolin, Viola, *Improvisation for the Theatre*, Northwestern University Press, Evanston, Illinois, 1963.

DIRECTING

Cole, Toby and Chinoy, Helen Krich, *Directors on Directing*, Peter Owen, London, 1964

Fernald, John, *Sense of Direction*, Secker and Warburg, London, 1968.

Miles-Brown, John, *Directing Drama*, Peter Owen, London, 1980.

VOICE

Berry, Cecily, *The Voice and the Actor*, Harrap, London, 1973.

Turner, J. Clifford, *Voice and Speech in the Theatre*, revised by Malcolm Morrison, Pitman, London, 1977.

MOVEMENT

Pisk, Litz, *The Actor and His Body*, Harrap, London, 1975.

GENERAL

Artaud, Antonin, *The Theatre and Its Double*, Grove Press, New York, 1958.

Barrault, Jean-Louis, *The Theatre of Jean-Louis Barrault*, Barrie and Rockliff, London, 1961.

Brook, Peter, *The Empty Space*, Macgibbon and Kee, London, 1968.

Esslin, Martin, *Brecht: A Choice of Evils*, Mercury Books, London, 1965.

Grotowski, Jerzy, *Towards a Poor Theatre*, Eyre Methuen, London, 1975.